HEAD FOR THE HIGH COUNTRY

David Caffey

HEAD FOR THE HIGH COUNTRY

David L. Caffey

ABINGDON PRESS
Nashville · New York

Library of Congress Cataloging in Publication Data

CAFFEY, DAVID L 1947-   Head for the high country.
1. Philmont Scout Ranch.
2. Camping—New Mexico. I. Title.
GV196.P48C3   796.54'22   72-6087

ISBN 0-687-16730-2

MANUFACTURED BY THE PARTHENON PRESS AT
NASHVILLE, TENNESSEE, UNITED STATES OF AMERICA

foreword

How proud the late Waite Phillips would have been of Dave Caffey . . . and the hundreds of others who have served on the Philmont staff.

These are the young men who grow up and find themselves in the beautiful and majestic land that he gave to the boys of America. After all, this was the primary motivation of his gift to the Boy Scouts of America—a gift consisting of more than 127,000 acres and the prestigious Philtower Building in the heart of Tulsa, Oklahoma. The spirit of this magnificent gift is emblazoned in bronze:

> These properties
> are donated and dedicated
> to the Boy Scouts of America
> for the purpose of perpetuating
> faith, self-reliance, integrity, and freedom,
> principles used to build this great country
> by the American pioneer.

So that
these future citizens may
through thoughtful guidance
and by the inspiration of nature
visualize and form a code of living
to diligently maintain these high ideas
and our proper destiny.

—Waite Phillips
Dec. 31, 1941

Dave Caffey has articulated eloquently his love and affection for Philmont. Through thoughtful guidance and by the inspiration of nature, Philmont has affected his life in the positive manner that Waite Phillips envisioned.

The thousands of campers—high school aged young men—who come to Philmont each summer for their high adventure capture the same spirit so ably expressed here.

Philmont staff and campers, Scout leaders, and all camp related people will find much of themselves in this delightful, fascinating account.

Head for the High Country could well be dedicated to Mrs. Genevieve Phillips, wife of the late Waite Phillips, and to her son, Elliott. It will be most heartwarming for them to know that Philmont is achieving the spirit of this magnificent gift in the lives of growing boys. Those who come to Philmont do become better men for themselves and for America.

Joe Davis
Director of Camping
Philmont Scout Ranch

preface

This is about a stretch of mountain country that started out as just a place. Through the summer days and across the seasons, though, it has become more than that to many of the ones who have roamed its ridges and canyons. It is only an uncivilized piece of country, but something is there that can touch a person.

When I first came into the country of the Philmont Scout Ranch, it was from a world where a life-span was something that came in a neat package, precisely styled and sealed in plastic. It was a clear-cut matter to get on the program that had already been laid out for you and take each of the steps that followed one after another as surely as B follows A. There was some kind of invented system for everything. Adventure then was some quality that had left with the older days, something that people could now only try to know in fiction or maybe experience from a pill. What was left was a world that was controlled and efficient—and dull.

The summer days changed that. In those summers I began to think that there might be something more to look for. Those days somehow brought me closer to an earth that was real and good. I began to discover a few simple goods that satisfied more than all the entertaining gadgets and conveniences a factory could turn out. I discovered self-dependence and time that flowed without calibrations, and a kind of beauty that appeared in the absence of invented things. I met people. The days were not loaded in advance, but the sun would come up and there a day would be, and by dusk it had proved its worth.

Many thousands of men and boys and young men have come through those summer days, and have left them to go back down into the world that is. Sooner or later they all leave the mountains, but they don't all leave the high country.

David L. Caffey

acknowledgments

Many of the historical references included in this book reflect the contributions of Dr. Jerry Traut and Dr. Lawrence Murphy. Both served Philmont for many summers and were responsible for uncovering much of the regional history which has become embedded in the lore of Philmont. Dr. Murphy is the author of two excellent volumes of history on the Philmont area.

Mr. Joe Davis followed the development of this book and was most generous with help and encouragement.

*Here, deep in the heart of the primitive forest where wild-
life abounds and nature's wonders challenge the imagination, those Scouts whose experience and training have
qualified them for this adventure in the wilderness will
be able to have the experiences of our pioneer forefathers
who established the traditions and the historical back-
ground of this high country.*

> —Committee of the National Council,
> Boy Scouts of America, accepting
> the gift of Waite Phillips, 1939

1

The hills of home—Trail Peak, Urraca Mesa, Black Mountain, Baldy. They lie in a jagged range of craggy ridges and timbered lobes that starts in the lower chain of the Rockies and reaches toward Colorado. The skyline that they form belongs to the Philmont Scout Ranch, and it traces what surely must be one of the most beautiful works of geography anywhere. A 214-square-mile hunk of northeastern New Mexico, Philmont is a national Scout

wilderness domain, the gift of oilman Waite Phillips to the
Boy Scouts of America.

A small settlement of Scouting professionals and tradesmen stays at the foot of the mountains through the snows,
but Philmont lives for the summer. Early in June the
staff men begin showing up—most of them from colleges
and universities, some from teaching jobs—and when all
of them have come in, they amount to some four hundred.
The first week is spent in training and settling in, and
after that it is Katie-bar-the-door. For the rest of the
summer planes fly into Colorado Springs, trains roll into
Raton, and buses and cars roll up to Philmont's reception
dock bringing boys at the rate of three hundred a day.
They come from everywhere.

The boys who come to Philmont come looking for a
little more than just a place where they can sleep on a
cot and eat in a dining hall and learn to tie knots. They
have had all that. They are at least fourteen and have
been Scouts for a long time. Most of them have come on
money that they have saved up and that could have gone
for a lot of other things, and more often than not they
have crossed half the country to get here. They are looking
for Scouting at its natural best. They are looking for
country like they have never seen from a car window or
on a TV screen. They are looking for adventure. Will
they find it? You bet they will. It's out there.

Out there is the mountain country. It is a vast and
overbearing country, too big to be taken in at the first
look, as a flatland or city might be. Beyond the first
ridge which separates you is that wilderness of unseen
mountains. There is always something beyond, and the
promise that it would be worth taking a look at. There
are deep canyons where one way goes ahead and two
sides go up. There are windblown peaks that put you

above the world. There are trails that wind across forested slopes through towers of deep green pine and fir. Grassy open meadows and cool shaded parklands are nestled in among the high reaches. Countless chilled streams course their way down from the high springs, rarely very big and never dry, but ever gurgling down. The cool mountain air drifts in clean, pine-touched breezes. There is enough mountain country that each of the daily twenty or thirty crews can pick a different route, cover five to ten miles a day, camp at a different place every night, and still each not see but a small stretch of Philmont.

The Scouts come in contingents organized by their own leaders in their local areas. Some of them come by charter flights. Some groups have their own buses and tour their way across the country and back. Some local councils bring up to three or four hundred or more boys in a summer. Other groups are made up of a few boys and a leader who have come out in one car. Each group is met at the reception dock by a Ranger who is the guide for the first few days. A mountain expedition gets to be a kind of personalized thing between a boy and his friends and the country around them. It is not the kind of trip you can enjoy with a mob, so the treks are made in trail crews of about ten boys and their adult leaders from home. After a half day of registration and processing, the Ranger gets them outfitted for the trail and they are gone to the hills for a ten-day pack trip.

When a bus lets the crew off at one of several starting points scattered across the front of the mountains, the boys are on their own. Everything they will need to get along is in the packs that ride high behind their shoulders. They have some pots, lightweight trail tents, their bedrolls, a change of clothes, a first-aid kit, and maybe an ax or bow saw. Each boy has a deep plate and a spoon to eat out of, and a poncho to keep the rain off. They have a supply of trail food packets and will pick up more of the dehydrated meals at commissaries along the way. What they don't have is the ton of clothing and equipment the Ranger told them to leave behind. They don't need it. They will spend the next week and a half hiking around forty to sixty miles of the backcountry and doing whatever they find to do out there. Whatever the weather does during that time, they will know about it.

Through the backcountry are scattered the mountain camps. Where the terrain levels out enough for pitching tents and where there is a water supply, there is a camp. Some camps, like Abreu, Ponil, and Fish Camp, are set in along canyon floors beside fresh running streams. Some, like Miners Park and Black Mountain Camp, are in wooded highland parks, the campsites scattered through a thick, shaded forest. Beaubien and Miranda are high meadow camps located where rolling, grassy, open spaces interrupt the mountainsides. Many of the camps are trail camps with only a rock fire lay, some even ground where tents might be pitched, and maybe a spring. Twenty or so others have some kind of settlement where there is a staff of three to ten living for the summer.

There is always something to do in the camps. In the low areas of the Baldy country where there used to be placer mining, you can take an old-style, heavy gauge gold pan down on Ute Creek and pan for gold flecks, or you could hike around to French Henry and take a tour into a shaft of the Aztec Mine, which is still inspected and kept shored up. Down at Fish Camp in the far southern country a boy can tie his own trout fly, then go down to the Rayado and catch supper on it. At Urraca Camp groups can do some mountaineering—with ropes and pitons and carabiners and a climbing instructor, they can climb some of the mesa's crags and rappel down the outcrops. At Ponil a crew of boys can pick up a couple of burros, learn to fit a packsaddle on them, load their kyack boxes, throw a diamond hitch over the packs, and then let the burros carry some of their gear while the boys lead them through the north country. At Indian Writings, Scouts work alongside archaeologists in the "dig," excavating the homesites of prehistoric Indians and sifting for evidence and artifacts. Or the boys can hike Baldy or Mount Phillips. Or learn to use the kind of old cap and ball rifles that provided game for the earliest trappers in these parts. Or ride a horse along the green draw of Hidden Valley. Or explore.

The mountains are full of wildlife. Mule deer are plentiful. Clusters of doe and velvet bucks come down into the meadows to graze in early morning and at sundown. They are light-footed and silent. Their bodies move with the flow of one tawny muscle, trim and lean and fit. The deer get used to seeing people down in their grasslands and they will stay to graze even with boys around watching and taking pictures. But they are also high-strung and sensitive, hardly ever relaxing the keen, taut twitch in their ears. And whenever a man comes too close or something just feels too close, they are off and bounding to the hills. The antler-crested bucks mostly stay to the higher, less traveled reaches.

Black bear also range the mountain country, although they live more as loners and are less social than the deer. Bears stay out of the way in the heat of the day, but by night they are on the prowl in an endless hunt for food. Sometimes they will drift into camps, following the scent of campers' food. Some bears have made camps their habitual summer feeding grounds and can be expected to appear about dark every day. Bears have no trouble narrowing down a smell to where the food is, and most of them are rangy about getting at it, so that a Scout group that has any sense will spend a little time each evening rigging a safe place for their supplies. At the front of the mountains, stretching eastward over the grassy plain, is the fenced-off range of Philmont's buffalo herd. Although they are not completely ready to become pets, the buffalo have become pretty docile in their pasture; once or twice a year they might go on a tear and run through a couple of fences for old times' sake.

The rest of the wild creatures stay back in the sticks and will have nothing to do with people. The slender pronghorn antelope that graze in the low grasslands before the mountains are even more skittish than the deer and will spring for brush cover at the slightest approach of a human. Flocks of wild turkey are around in several parts of the ranch, but are hardly ever seen. An elk herd roams Wilson Mesa, one of the last retreats in a land where they used to wander more at ease. Early morning hikers coming up from Pueblano may get a glimpse of the elk watering at dawn, but more often the only trace left for men to see is an occasional old antler rack, reminder of a proud and powerful buck that once was. In the high meadow country just beyond Philmont's far south corner boundary is the forgotten rangeland where herds of wild horses roamed in recent times, and some of them may still be there. Least seen of all are the few mountain lions that pace the least-traveled ridges in the farthest backcountry.

The land of Philmont has the kind of history that only a wild and open land like this can have. It is a past that has not been relegated to books, but has been absorbed by the country itself, leaving faded pieces of time that remain very much at the surface of the land now. The Santa Fe

Trail is still there, long since grown over beyond easy recognition but still there—the flat stretch just before the mountains where ox teams labored a long time ago. On the banks of the Rayado, in a flat grove where the mountain growth extends a little out onto the plains, is a restoration of Kit Carson's home. There, at what is now the Rayado training camp, Carson lived for a time, doing some sheep ranching and trading supplies to pioneers traveling out the Santa Fe Trail.

Up north, prehistoric Indians left their petroglyphs among the rocky ledges and overhangs of North Ponil Canyon. The symbols, mostly sets of concentric circles, are chipped into the rock and sometimes colored to a black or dark reddish hue by fire or some substance. Two of the ancient dwellings have been excavated and a great many bones and relics have been unearthed in the digging and sifting that is carried on daily in the summer by the archaeologists and their Scout helpers.

Baldy's slopes tell of a gold-mining life that set the mountain ablaze, then flickered and died, finally leaving the green woods to grow over the ruins. Left upon a now lush mountainside are the crumbling foundations of a couple of gold mills and the scattered entrances to tumbled-in mine shafts. At the foot of the great mountain is the residue of a ghost town, Baldy Town, which is now a Philmont camp. The stories of gold and the men who sought it in the Black Horse, the Aztec, and the Deep Tunnel mines are there and yet alive in the decaying evidence that marks their truth.

Up Turkey Canyon are the rotting timbers of the cabin Black Jack Ketchum's gang fled to after holding up a train, there to shoot it out with Sheriff Farr and his posse. Turkey Canyon was about the first mountain cove you would come to riding hell-bent from Twin Mountains, and that's where the outlaws turned in to take to the hills. When they rode out again, Farr was dead and Sam Ketchum's arm was blown open with a wound that would finish him off in Santa Fe prison with blood poisoning.

Grown over but still discernible is the roadbed of the Cimarron and Northwestern, whose freight cars long years ago rolled out of Ponil Canyon loaded with fresh-cut timber from the tall pine slopes of Skyline Ridge and the Ponil country. Near Pueblano Camp, ruins of the loggers' cabins lie in decay, their rock chimneys scattered where they fell.

The earthly surroundings, as intriguing as they can easily be, are not the only thing worth holding to about Philmont. The way of living that they make natural is at least as important. It is a style of living that, in a way, humbles the materialistic, structured pattern to which most of us hand ourselves over. Philmont's is a strenuous life, but a fairly simple one that is not cluttered with the devices to which we have become addicted as a fix for boredom or idleness out there in the mainstream.

Up in the mountains you come to appreciate a difference between what sorts of tasks are satisfying and what things are senseless motions. The worries up there are about getting three meals a day and having a dry place to sleep, not about appropriations and traffic snarls. Simple though the life is, time somehow never hangs heavy. Through long stretches of uncounted days in the mountains I have never found myself wanting for television and the papers and the dozens of devices we buy to entertain ourselves in the city. Each new day in the high country is important not in what reward the calendar has to offer for that day or for its juxtaposition to the approach of a weekend, but just for its own discoveries.

Although mountain life is not without occasional disappointments and frustrations of its own, it is largely un-burdened with the barrage of pointless activities that mark so much of our time in town. Every job in the hills has some intrinsic purpose to it—providing food, shelter, comfort—tasks whose satisfaction is direct. There are no lines to stand in, no cars to break down, no reams of forms to fill out. Neither is there any set of success objects that have to be sought and collected as proof of self-worthiness. The boys depend upon themselves and on their friends for survival, each one using the resources that he has. There is no need and no reward for pretension.

Philmont campers meet a raw and open country. They are not insulated from weather and wild creatures. They are not pressed into grooves of schedule and routine. Be-cause of this, because there is no automatic response to every alarm, no instant squelch for every squirm, there is room for things to happen and room for young men to deal with them in their own way. There is, in short, a lived adventure.

2

That first summer I was a Ranger. So were a hundred others. We based in Ranger City, a community of wall tents at one end of Camping Headquarters. There on the south flank of Tent City stood a double-row quadrangle of pale green tents mounted on wooden platforms, and in the middle of the square was a brown painted locker building. About the tents there were usually some Rangers waiting for their groups to come in, others sprawling around on days off between expeditions; and always there were a few sanding down ax handles and tinkering with their equipment. We each checked in there for a couple of days out of a five-day cycle to rest, reset for the trail, and pick up another new camping group.

I took thirteen groups out from headquarters and saw them on their way through the mountains. Like the rest of the Rangers, I met each crew at the reception dock where the groups checked in. First I would put them through a half-day routine of registration and details in headquarters. I took them to the camp office to sign in and to a place where we had their picture made. Then we walked down to the health lodge for medical inspections and over to the equipment quadrangle where we took out whatever gear we needed. Next I had them bring everything for the trek to a grassy place on the display terrace and we would get down to business. There they spread every imaginable item of clothing and equipment out on their ground cloths—all stuff they thought they were going to take—and I went around and showed each boy what he would and would not want to carry over fifty miles of mountains. I discarded hatchets and sheath knives and desert type, half-gallon canteens, and some of those flashlights with a searchlight on top and a ten-pound power cell under it. By the time I was through, each one would have a suitable pack that he could haul without too much trouble.

On their second day at Philmont, we had a trip mapped out and were ready for the trail. We waited at the loading dock with our packs, and soon a yellow Cimarron school bus would pull around to take us out to a starting point. The old bus driver would waddle down, grinning at everybody in sight and brandishing his bay window around as he supervised the equipment loading. "Hello, Red," he would chortle, throwing his hand my way in a half wave.

He was Earl Swope, a jovial man who could have passed for Santa Claus. Earl was a local cattle and school bus baron, and if he wasn't the one driving, another of his family would be. Earl had a fleet of a dozen or more buses at Philmont, most of them driven by Swopes or in-laws. For twenty or thirty minutes we rode out a dirt road and watched the land out the window, maybe thinking briefly of the comforts and conveniences that were left far behind. Soon the bus would turn into a loop of the road and grind down to a stop. We unloaded the packs and watched the bus weave back onto the road and move out of sight toward headquarters.

Each boy boosted his pack onto a knee, looped his arms through the straps, and jiggled the load into place on his back, this time for real. For most of the summer the first that I would see of a region was when I landed there with a group, so we would pull out a topographical map, set it in agreement with the lay of the land, and locate the way to the starting camp. We ciphered its maze of bench marks and concentric lines, and sure enough there would be some kind of trail leading off in the direction of the camp. We would file onto it and hike it to its end. Some crews would soon be faltering and gasping at the thin, high air as we started up into the mountains, so we stopped often for short breathers and pack breaks.

If the first day's camp was an inhabited one, a staff man would come out to meet us and to show us the camping spots. If it was a trail camp we were on our own, and would just locate the water supply and then find a level place to camp nearby. I generally filled the boys in on a few peculiarities about mountain camping, like which direction to set the tents to be sure that they would stand in the canyon drafts. I talked about the erosion that could come of ditching tents and showed the boys how to use a dining fly to their advantage in wet weather. After we had our camp set up, I would show them the right way to use an ax and bow saw and remind them that it was plenty important to use them right, given the distances they would be from medical help. If there was some good activity provided in the camp we would get the boys into it, and then I went off exploring in the mountain country that fascinated me so. If the afternoon was long I usually ended up on some ridge or up a stream or poking around some kind of old ruins.

We would start supper pretty early. The dry trail-food packets and pine wood fires were new and strange to most of the groups, so cooking and cleaning up were bound to take a while. I learned early in the summer to allow at least a half hour for getting together the aluminum pots and utensils that were dispersed among the boys' packs and that were somehow easy to lose track of.

Most of the boys were skeptical of the trail food, which was something different from anything that had ever turned up on their tables at home. Many of the grizzly, middle-aged leaders came in at the end of a trek showing off the two or three notches they had taken up in their belts. But I grew to like the stuff and gained weight on it. In fact, headquarters food was such that I looked forward to getting out on the trail where I could get plenty to eat. Out there the campers were shy of the strange meals and would not really be starved enough to eat them for a day or two, so that is where I would eat well. The meals came dry out of plastic bags, went into water, and were boiled, so there wasn't much in the way of a meat or salad. There usually was some kind of casserole mix, a couple of freeze-dried vegetables, biscuit or cornbread mix, and a dessert. The first night on the trail I would have some cans of peaches along; I'd get a dutch oven, mix up a cobbler, set the oven down in burning coals, and heap hot red coals on top. It was with the turnout of the cobbler that I gained the favor or the wrath of the group.

When the sun went down on us, the summer day would turn into a cool, almost chilling night. We'd have to hurry to have the dishes and pots scrubbed and rinsed and put away before the evening's light wore away. Then we took our jackets and walked up to the campfire place where we would get ourselves situated on a log and join the rest of the groups in camp to hear the "Philmont Story," a campfire tale put on at all of the starting camps. The story was about the land and the men who had worked it—prehistoric Indians, fur trappers, miners, ranchers, Scouts. By the time it ended with Philmont's song, the night's chill was setting in and the boys headed back for their bedrolls. The group leader and I usually stopped, though, to have a cup of hot coffee with the staff and the other leaders, and often there was a character or two among them who would keep us listening into the night.

When the long day's journey caught up with us, we stumbled back to camp, testing our way through the dark trees, having of course neglected to bring a flashlight to the campfire. I'd crawl into my trail tent and set a match to my candle. I would squirm around between the close canvas tent sides spreading a plastic sheet over the cold, dewey ground, then start the day's last job of blowing up my air mattress. I shucked my Scout clothes in the cool night air and groped in my pack for a T-shirt that I hoped the evening dampness hadn't gotten to first. Finally I buttoned the tent flaps, crawled between the flannel layers of the sleeping bag, then blew a gust at the candle flame. The woods noises would keep me on edge for a while, then I slept.

At first light we were up and going on breakfast. The

boys came shivering out of their tents to huddle around the good roaring fire that was the center of camp life. They were clad in ragtag layers of whatever clothes could be uncovered to warm them against the damp morning chill. Their heads were tousled and sleepy. Breakfast tasted extra good on the trail, partly because the smell of bacon frying and pancake syrup heating came through so pure and delicious in the thin, untampered mountain air, and partly because breakfast was the one meal whose quality was not much altered by the requirements of trail packaging. In the mountains there always seemed to be a ridge in the way of the morning sun, so it would be a while before it rose enough to shine its warmth on the campsite. We let the tents stand until the sun could take the dew off them, and by the time they were struck and folded and packed away, the breakfast cleanup was all done and we were ready to hike out.

On that second day out we would get away from the foothills and service roads and would hike a trail winding up into higher mountain country. The boys began to see how they could navigate their way across the countryside with maps and compasses, and they started to notice canyons and peaks and marks that would tell them where they were. I hiked behind and was pretty much along for the scenery, just seeing that the group would be able to take care of itself all right. If the hike was over four or five miles, we would spend half the day out on the trail. Noon often found us sprawled around on top of a mountain spreading peanut butter on pilot biscuit and cutting off slices of canned meat with a pocket knife. Sometimes we would take a hiking break and use the rest stop to get out the first-aid kit and doctor any new blisters the hike had produced. When we got to our camp, the tents went up and we settled in without much bother. Some of the boys would go off to see what they could find and a few others would build a fire under a bucket of water and start washing out their trail-crusted socks, and I would know that they were getting the feel of life on the trail.

The next morning after breakfast we parted company, the Scouts to be on their way to their next camp and I to find my way back to headquarters. I had the whole day to get back in, so sometimes I would hike in by some part of the country I hadn't seen. If I had things to do back at headquarters and was in a hurry to get there, I would head for the nearest road and hope to meet up with a bus or commissary truck, or I might end up bouncing in on the back of a dump truck with a load of garbage. When I got back to headquarters I'd stop at the Ranger office and lean my pack against the yellow stucco building, then swing the screen door open and greet Mr. Dunn, who would want to know how everything was going. After I had written up the usual page report, I looped my pack strap over one arm and headed for Tent City and the shower house to wash off the grimy trail feeling that was out of place in civilization. The following day was a day off. I could hike or do errands or go into town to eat a good meal and ogle the waitresses, and the day after that I was in the office after breakfast, ready to meet a new group and start all over.

I liked being a Ranger. We were a special breed among the men of Philmont. It took no longer than a few days for the younger ones to sense that it meant something to be a Ranger. We were a corps with a way that had lasted across the separate summers. We had a pride and a spirit that the more fragmented groups of the staff couldn't have. Over four hundred staff men were hired for the summer, but Rangers were among the few of those who ever really got to Philmont. Many of the others worked regular hours in headquarters at jobs like clerking and food service, and they lived in plaster bunkhouses or in tents that sat in rows out on an open lot. A Ranger was given a responsibility and he did it on his own. A lot of things were strictly up to him, and his groups' experiences depended upon what he did on his own volition out in the mountains. A Ranger knew what went into doing the job and recognized those among his peers who really knew the ways of the trail.

Most every Ranger had a Ranger look about him. A Ranger wore the same official uniform as any other staff man, same forest green or khaki summer shirt, same Scout khaki shorts, but on the Ranger it look functional, not ornamental. It was tough and stood up against the months of hard wear it got on the trail. Sticking out of the hip pocket would be a folded Philmont map, its layers pressed into a sweaty, body-molded state. The Ranger hiked in well-made ankle-top boots, well broken, over double layers of sweat socks. He soon wore a tawny, sun-baked look and an unstyled head of hair. He walked with a long, muscled gait that was conditioned from mountain miles under a backpack. But he never looked so much like a Ranger as when he was marinated in a film of sweat and soot and trail dust. That was a Ranger.

In many ways a Ranger lives the rambling boy life that he has at some time thought of. He comes to feel easy with any of a wide variety of groups and leaders, knows them briefly and is one of them for a few days, then is gone again. He lives out of a pack, and sundown hardly ever finds him in the same place twice. He sleeps on the ground, not as a weekend novelty a few times a year, but as his own familiar bed at the end of a day. He lives on trail food scooped out of a tin plate, and he eats without too much regard for a few ashes or a little grit that may find its way into the food. He is at home in the mountain world, tuned in on the feelings of its weather and its day span. The Ranger wants little in the way of possessions, but what things he does have are part of him—his pack, his boots, his tent. He learns the trails and canyons of the mountain country; he sees how the earth folds and learns where passage lies among the formations. He goes out looking for the high country.

Rangering made a good summer. I camped with groups from all over the country and I got to know some Scouters and men who were worth knowing. I saw a lot of Philmont, a lot of its mountain country and of the various jobs I might like doing there. The Ranger life took me to places I had never been and, in subtle ways, maybe changed my outlook more than I knew.

A Cimarron, New Mexico, school bus rolled down the straight road between quaking rows of trees on either side. Hail beat against the roof, and I looked out the window and wondered if this was Philmont. I didn't recognize anybody else on the bus, and I didn't recognize any of the country outside. There was nothing in sight that I could identify with the Texas flatland of my home, and I asked myself what it was that had made me so sure that I wanted to spend a summer out here. Before I got an answer, the bus wheeled in through a gateway, continued across a gravel parking lot, and came to a stop by a big covered porch where a sign read, "Reception Center—Welcome to Philmont." Three more buses pulled in behind us, and a couple hundred guys got out and began darting around, piling baggage on the loading dock. I mostly just stood there for a while, because I wasn't too sure what was going on. One of the few things I did know was that I was what was known as a Ranger, and I wouldn't have known that except that it said so on the contract I had gotten in the mail at home. I heard two or three guys say something about "Ranger," so I picked up my bags and followed them to a village of wall tents around a locker building.

The ones I was following found themselves an empty tent and moved in, so I did likewise. I kind of arranged my stuff around one of the army bunks, and pretty soon a spindly, crew-cut kid stuck his head in and asked was the other place empty. I said it was, so we shook hands and he moved his stuff in. We put on our Scout clothes and walked down to the dining hall for the summer's opening banquet. There were hundreds of staff men milling around on the lawn, more, it seemed, than Philmont could possibly have jobs for. There was a good enough meal, followed by a program of introductions of Scout officials—National Director of this and that to infinity. We walked back to Ranger City not knowing a whole lot more about our jobs than before. We hoped tomorrow we would find out what a Ranger was.

And we did. We filed through the lines for breakfast at daybreak, wincing a little at the early morning chill that would hang over New Mexico a couple of weeks into the summer. After that, no hour of daylight would be wasted in making Rangers out of the hundred strange faces that had come together. The new ones were assembled on rows of logs that were part of a chapel behind the grounds of Tent City, and the leaders set in to get us organized.

C. E. Dunn was the Chief Ranger, and when he began to speak, the first-timers could see that we were into a summer that would take us beyond the ordinary experiences. Mr. Dunn had lived his way into something of a slight legend, so that many had heard his name and, "You'll like him." Seventy years into his life, Clarence Dunn was leading a corps that he dearly loved, that was the work of his own hand and his own straight character. Mr. Dunn had served youth at Philmont for twenty summers and had led the Rangers since their beginning. Now that he was retired from his work as a school principal, the Rangers were his life. There was a gentleness about the man when he spoke to his Rangers, but that manner never cushioned the straight-ahead ideals that were in his mind. Mr. Dunn was not at Philmont to gaze at the mountains and enjoy the relaxation that his years entitled him to; he was there because he was forever in the business of helping young men to grow. Mr. Dunn spoke words that were lucid and simple. The man came straight across to the high school and college men who were two generations younger. The neatly trimmed appearance of his white hair and Scouter's uniform said nothing about him that was not so. Here, for a few hundred young men to know, was an honest man.

Mr. Dunn told us what would be happening in the next days and organized the mass of strangers into several training crews. The older Training Rangers took charge of their crews of the younger, uncertain ones and told them what kind of life to expect of Ranger training. Then they took their Rangers and wandered among the lodges and service areas and all of the places in headquarters that a Ranger would need to know. After lunch the hundred who would be Rangers laced on hike boots and lugged their backpacks to the broad porch of the bus dock.

The bus ride to Ponil gave us some idea of the dimensions of Philmont. We drove back down the highway, past the elegant Villa Philmonte that had been Waite Phillips' commanding ranch home, past the old polo barns, past the buffalo pasture, and through Cimarron. At the other side of the little town we turned off onto a dirt road and weaved along for another half hour, winding our way up a long canyon between some low ridges. We crossed through a corner of the famed CS Ranch, then the Chase Ranch and the old WS, then got back onto Philmont land and finally ended up at Ponil Base Camp, eighteen road miles from where we had started. We had traveled maybe half the length of Philmont.

Ponil was a sprawling base camp that covered easily two miles of the floor of Ponil Canyon where two forks of the creek come together. "Five Points," it had once been called, because of the five canyon trails that met there. Before that, the area had been a tiny French settlement, and the historic name of the canyon and its surrounding country derived from that fact. Ponil had been the headquarters of the old Philturn Rockymountain Scout Camp, and most of the old structures stood along the canyon sides. There were a couple of log houses, horse barns, and corrals, and a board commissary building. There were also the "Long House" and a dining lodge, both built of stout Oregon logs. Up the canyon were twenty or more campsites scattered along the river bottom.

The Ranger outfit was settling into Ponil for four days of camping and training. We would be getting used to life on the trail—living out of tents and supplying our own wood and water, and boiling up our own suppers from the strange dehydrated packets. During the days the crews would gather for sessions with specialists who knew about as much as there was to know of wilderness camping, first aid, orienteering, and safety training. We would get to know something of the country we were in—its trees and grasses and the life that grew among them. On one day the crews would each catch a couple of burros from the pasture and learn to saddle them, then throw a hitch over our gear and trek over Hart's Peak to Indian Writings for the night. Hazy smoke would be rising from a dozen campfires up the canyon before the sun took the chill out of the mountain air every day, and we would be going all day. And when we were done, we would all be Rangers.

Will Hobbs got the crew together and we took over one of the campsites that set in against the canyon wall. We worked along for a while at getting our food together and our tents comfortable, and soon it was time to cook supper. The trail food came out of plastic packets in dried chips of potatoes, carrots, beef, and anything else that could be dehydrated or freeze-dried. There were only two recipes: pour into water and boil, or boil water and pour into package. Because the mountain conifers would burn away to ashes, we soaped up the cooking pots and set them down into the open flames.

Just as we were going pretty well, a lazy cloud bank rolled up and began to water the canyon. Without even the fanfare of a thunderclap, the wet drops just started to fall. We all got out our ponchos and pitched a dining fly over the fire. From then on we were not picnicking; we were camping. Will knew his way across the Philmont trails, and he mentioned that a light afternoon shower was typical of the summer weather in these parts. We stood around in the smoke for another hour, and finally tasted a meal of gooey chicken a la king over some pasty biscuits. None of us wrote to cancel Diners' Club cards or fire our mothers. We did have some cans of peaches, from which Will whipped up a cobbler. Cobbler expertise was one of the marks of a true Ranger, and Will proved he was one, fiddling with the crust and sprinkling spices until it was just right. We got the dishes washed and trudged through the mud to the old dining hall for an evening meeting, and rain kept falling.

As the canyon went to bed, rain still came in a hard slant drizzle, and rain tapped at the tent canvas to get us up for Wednesday morning. The canyon was gray, and as we crawled out and looked the day over, there was no horizon that promised an end to the rain. Camping became tedious. Our boots were soaked and our clothes were wet and our sleeping bags were muggy with the moisture that was into everything. Everything had turned to water. We tramped out through the high grass looking for wood, and rain trickled over us where it would. The axes stuck between swollen fibers when we tried to split the firewood, and it burned only with constant fanning and coaxing. Noxious smoke filled the little space where we huddled under the tarp. Overhead there was still no seam in the gray wall, and misty rain washed all the color out of the hillsides. We stood around glum.

Down the rainy canyon moved a row of poncho raincoats. Through the drizzle drifted the tune,

> It ain't a gonna rain no more, no more;
> It ain't a gonna rain no more.
> How in the hell can the old folks tell,
> It ain't a gonna rain no more?

Another crew passed by chanting a crew yell, and we followed them down singing a song of our own. The lodge was giving off a festive clamor when we hung our dripping slickers and waded into the sea of Rangers that crowded across the broad floor. A good roaring fire blazed high in the fireplace and the place rocked with the cadence of rowdy camp songs.

Bill Wadsworth had charge of Ranger training. Wadsworth, a National Scout camping man, dominated the long room. He stood taller than any other man around, and he had the brawny look of an outdoorsman. He was full of energy and full of songs and full of Scouting, and it was impossible to be lethargic when he was running things. At mealtimes Wadsworth would go striding through the boggy camps in his waist-length parka, looking things over and seeing what might be done better. He knew all of the time-savers and safety precautions and was ever looking for better ways. When Mr. Wadsworth stopped in to talk, we would all listen. Although it was his occupation, camping had not become stale or routine to the man. Though he had been there many times, he was sharing something that brought him back to the Philmont country with those of us who were seeing most of it for the first time.

After the hundred had crowded in and settled to the floor, Wadsworth told the roomful of Rangers that we were going to see a flood. Radio and phone messages had reached Philmont telling of heavy rains that ranged over a wide area of the Southwest. Highways already had been washed out in Denver. With that said, we went ahead about the business of becoming Rangers.

As soon as lunch was cleared away, thunderbolts reverberated through the canyon and the gray sky wall burst with a violent new downpour. Most of the campsites sat scattered along the canyon floor in the low flats on either side of the creek, and before long, Wadsworth and Mr. Dunn had passed the word for them to be cleared out. The pouring rain made us hurry as we stuffed the wet clothes and pots in our packs and stole time to clean the place up. We filed out of the campsite and waded down to the creek, made a last crossing over the bridge there, and hiked down through the bog to the Long House, where we moved in with two other crews while the rest of the Rangers found shelter in the other permanent structures.

Ponil Creek was by now a debris-filled torrent, and its edges lapped up over the banks and into some of the campsites. Logs up to a couple of feet across came bounding through the turbulent waters. Now and then one would be tossed high and jar the narrow footbridges; eventually the hard battering ripped the bridges out of their banks and sent them hurtling unheeded down the canyon.

The new place provided just enough space for people wall to wall. The night scene found the floors covered with overlapped sleeping bags, groups gathered around card games and camp games and bull sessions. Late in the evening the oldest Training Ranger mustered the crowd around the fireplace. Its wispy flames provided the room's only light. He talked for a little about the day's events and about what it meant to be a Ranger, and the group got quiet and listened to what the old Ranger had to say. He then unreeled the most effective ghost story I have ever heard, climaxing it with a wild screeching leap into the crowd. Outside, it rained.

When another day came, we waded to the old lodge for breakfast and more training. Bill Wadsworth told the Ranger corps that the waters throughout the region were on the rise, and we would have to get out of Ponil Canyon and back to headquarters. The mountain country was steep and usually arid, so the rains ran off the slopes in tremendous volumes that had begun to overpower the watershed and tear away at the banks and waterways. The buses that had brought us in to be trained would not be back to get us out. Ponil Creek, charging full and parallel to the canyon road, had torn chunks of earth out of the road. We would hike down the canyon to a place nine miles away where the buses could meet us.

The rain had slackened for a couple of hours during the morning, but it was with us as we packed to start the long march out. One by one the Ranger crews were checked off to start down the boggy canyon, while a few leaders hung behind to see that everyone was out and to secure the buildings as they could. The brigade that marched down through the rainy, gray veil was a tattered one. Some were draped in ponchos, some had flimsy nylon windbreakers that clung to them, and others wore raincoats that were made for city walking and that left their packs to be soaked in the rain. All afternoon the long pilgrimage moved along through sloppy mud and the constant drizzle, slowed because part of the road was under water and other parts were gone. In a few hours four yellow spots appeared distant in the deep gray mist. We slogged on to where a deep gorge severed the road, a pool of soft mud at its bottom. We waded on through and stood to knock globs of mud off our boots and clothes before loading onto the buses. Almost every Ranger was caked to his knees, and some had fallen in the mud and were good and muddy the rest of the way up. Trashed or not though, most of the crews came in bantering and singing the songs that had sounded along the canyon all the afternoon.

Between the Ranger buses and headquarters, between us and a meal and a shower and dry clothes, lay a nine-mile stretch of road and the Cimarron River. We made the highway and cruised into town, then the buses ground to a halt before an emergency scene at the Cimarron. The river had always been a little mountain stream narrow enough to hop across. Now it was a torrential gushing floodtide, raging down the canyon and cutting an unbelievable sixty-yard swath out of its banks. Lines of ten or twenty cars stood backed up along the road on either side, and the only visible motion aside from the rage of the Cimarron was the disappearing flow of the cars' exhaust trails and the oscillation of windshield wipers.

Police and highway patrol cars stood parked by the

bridge, and state troopers patrolled the crossing. A small group of official-looking men deliberated on the bridge, and talk spread that they had declared the bridge unsound and closed it to traffic. After a time the bus drivers got back on, and while the cars waited in rows on the highway shoulders, four buses of Philmont's Rangers crept past them and across the bridge. A day later, that bridge was gone and traffic into the ranch was shut off altogether. A short drive brought us home to the broad, rustic layout of Tent City. The buses pulled in across the puddly, water-logged lot and stopped before the dock, and the hundred dripping Rangers jumped down into the drizzle singing:

> I want to go back to Philmont
> Where the old Rayado flows,
> Where the rain comes a-seepin'
> In the tent where you're a-sleepin'
> And the water says, "Hello."
> I want to wake up in the mornin'
> With my socks all wringin' wet,
> For it brings back fondest memories
> That a Ranger can't forget.

By Friday morning a crisis was definitely on, and the few hundred now shelved in headquarters squeezed into the main dining hall to hear what things looked like. The summer was up in the air and groups huddled around rumors of what damage had passed and what would be done. The Director of Camping walked in and strode to the front, and the chatter thinned. Joe Davis stepped up on a folding chair, and there was silence across the room.

"And it rained for forty days and forty nights," he quoted. The tense hall exploded in cheers and laughter. When the clamor had subsided, Davis set out to tell his men what Philmont faced. All roads into Philmont were shut with washed-out bridges. Several buildings had been smashed, and Philmont's reservoirs were filled with debris and sediment. Two cars had been swept away, and a commissary driver had barely gotten out alive when the crest battered his truck away. Telephone lines all were down and the C.B. radios provided the only contact to the outside. One camp was ruined, its meadows overlaid with rock and gravel. Boulder train and logjams blocked many of the mountain canyons, and trails had been obliterated in many places. Vital systems to supply water, phones, and electricity to headquarters would have to be restored, and we could only hope that the state could fix the highway damage. Joe Davis thanked God that no life had been lost in the disaster; then he held his shiny bald head straight and flexed his tanned fist, and proclaimed that with the teamwork of a great Philmont staff, the ranch would be ready in one week. In the meantime, the thousand Scouts already on the road and bound for Philmont would have to be turned back—state troopers and local places across the country had already been contacted about that.

Life around headquarters was slow. The water piped in was murky and in short supply. All the drinking water was treated and the dining hall served on paper plates. We all went dirty. There were training meetings and free time for the Rangers. By Saturday a temporary bridge had been built over the Cimarron, and some of us made a junket into town.

Philmont's head men and national Scout officials burned their lamps late in planning for the rebuilding. Overseeing the work during the day and discussing new plans into the late hours, they went to many resources to line up the heavy equipment, construction supplies, and know-how that the job required. By Sunday they had something for the Rangers to do. The word was passed to get on our trashiest work clothes and show up at the loading dock. An assortment of jeeps, panel wagons, and pickups carried us up the road into the middle of Philmont and toward Cimarroncito Camp. We sidestepped deep ruts and splashed through puddles and came to a stop where the road disappeared into a small lake. The reason for our being there was plain to see. The creek had cut a great watery plain out across the road and the flats, and could not find its channel once the waters had gone down. The side of the creek where the spillover lay had to be built up to divert the water from its new course down the road so that the flow could be sent downstream.

The Ranger boys scattered out over the flood plain and waded in to work. Some crews got together and shouldered heavy logs, while others formed lines and passed rocks along to build up the dam, and still more filled sandbags and stacked them along the little seawall. The Rangers all played as they worked knee-deep in the flood waters, and the long dam took form. By the end of the morning it was big enough, and it took in the swollen stream as it was supposed to.

As the Rangers were put to work, so were the others around the ranch, who soon proved Philmont's manpower force something to be proud of. Philmont had permanent tradesmen in mechanics, carpentry, plumbing, and electricity—Philmont men—who lived there and were part of the place. Since they had installed most of the old facilities in each camp, the men already knew what was to be done and did it. The summer camp staffs were shipped out to their mountain places as soon as conditions were livable, each group supplied with tools and hardware for building new trail bridges and repairing what could be repaired.

One other thing holding up Philmont's opening was the destructive beating taken by the three hundred miles of wilderness trails. Even with the trails some of the Philmont country was plenty rugged, and at least some of the trails had been badly wrecked. Some trails would wind around the contours of a rock-strewn slope. Others rambled along creek bottoms and crossed narrow ledge passes where the stream had severed them. All the trails would have to be covered and made safe and passable before the Scout groups could be sent on a trip plan. The trail job would take a lot of able bodies, and the Rangers had that. "Operation Ranger" was handed over to C. E. Dunn and Bill Wadsworth, who mapped out segments of the trails and assigned their repair to a dozen or so trail crews of five or six Rangers.

The convoy of trucks that had taken us out for the flood-check work picked up the trail crews and scattered them over most of Philmont. We all took along an arsenal of axes and crosscut saws and surveyor's tape. Our little crew was dumped at the Chandler Canyon cutoff on the Ponil road. We strapped on our backpacks and were on our own. We hiked the winding jeep road up and over Chandler Pass and down into the brown and usually dry country of Dean Canyon. In a couple of places in the intricate pattern of switchbacks on Chandler Pass, road machinery would have to push the caved-in upper bank off what was supposed to be the road. Water normally ran through Dean Canyon like it would run off a roof, so although there was evidence of flooding in the boulder-filled streams and graveled flood plains, the canyon trail was hot and dusty now. But just about lunchtime we rounded a turn of the canyon and came upon something that satisfied our grimy faces.

In the middle of where the road was supposed to be, the flooded stream had scooped out a big clear pond. We stared through its crystal waters to a smooth rock bottom, and there was even a little grotto where the stream trickled in from a rocky overhang. Swimming in the streams was not an approved activity in these parts at all, since the streams were a main source of drinking water. Under the circumstances, though, we thought that Waite Phillips would not have objected to our washing up a little. We were out of our clothes and in the water, and stayed there for an extended lunch hour. The water was cool and stayed clear for as long as we splashed and floated and soaked in it. While we ate our trail lunch on the surrounding rocks, the crew leader took up his notebook and reluctantly noted the road damage that had caused the pool.

We hiked the last mile up the canyon to New Dean Camp, and there we set up for the night. We pitched the tents and fixed our trail supper, and took to our sleeping bags, tired, while the sun still shone down across the canyon. In the morning we were up and cooking just after four, determined to stay ahead of the north country's dry, rasping heat. We put in eight rugged miles along the sides of Bear Canyon, stopping sometimes to cut fallen logs and move brush and rock off the trail. Our early rising got us back to camp a little after lunchtime, and we headed straight for an afternoon in the pool.

Our last day on the trails was a good hard one. We scaled a ridge to get out of Dean Canyon, then headed down Turkey Canyon toward the highway. We left the trail once to climb to a piney summit where a fire control tower stood alone. We climbed the steps that wound up the swaying steel tower, entered the observation cubicle, and took a look at the maps and fire spotter devices inside. Back on the trail, we dropped into Turkey Canyon to start the long, dry hike out to the Cimarron highway. Turkey Creek was but a name, and there were no wells where we might get water. Neither were there shade trees along this long, straight canyon, and the sun beat down with a hard, burning glare. At least there were aesthetic features. Halfway down the canyon we came upon the rotting timbers of the cabin which had been the hideout of Black Jack Ketchum. We stood there to appreciate the wreckage, then hiked on down the parched canyon. We reached the highway and before too long a vehicle was there to pick us up. The driver said we must be miserably grimy after all those days out there working without showers. "Yeah," we answered.

Back at headquarters it seemed that Joe Davis' proclamation of a week ago had come to pass. Philmont would open. A lot of people had done a lot of work, and at least some kind of repair had been made to the vital things which had been ruined. A week after the confusion and ruin, Philmont was back together and ready for camping groups. Giff Kessler walked into the locker building and posted a notice. "6-21-65, The following Rangers will report to the Ranger office at 7:00 A.M. tomorrow 6-22." The third name down was mine, and I ambled out, glancing skyward for any foreboding of a light afternoon shower.

The groups I took out into the mountains were from all over the country and each one was different—from the Kingsport, Tennessee, outfit that was my first excursion after the flood to the summer's last trek with Mr. Munton, three times a Philmont trail leader.

One of the best outings I made was with a group from Illinois. The crew had two leaders, one of them a regular advisor for the crew, and the other the leader of their whole contingent from home. The contingent leader was Jim Stevenson, a Scout executive and camp director in the home council. He was around forty, active and friendly, and an easy leader. The boys really liked him. There were two older boys and a bunch of younger ones. They fell right in together and were a good outfit. They were prepared and organized, and they were looking for all that they had heard there was to do here.

When they showed up at the loading dock with their equipment ready for the ride out to Ponil, one of the older boys came carrying this pack frame with his regular pack attached and a bed-roll tied on below. Lashed on in a web of string behind them was a guitar jutting backward in an unbalanced overhang, its peg-head sticking far out to one side of the boy's head. I didn't recall seeing any guitar at the equipment shakedown, and I went into a harangue about the impracticality and foolishness of dragging something as large, as awkward, and as unnecessary as a guitar through the mountains. This was not a dude ranch or city park, I reiterated, but a long and rugged trail that would be the end of his guitar. It would end up as kindling wood, I guessed. Jim spoke up to say that he had just happened to come by the guitar from a music store friend of his who had dragged it out of a junk room in the back of the store and offered it for the boys to take along and plunk around on. It was a sorry guitar anyway, he said, so they didn't especially care what happened to it. I looked back at him askance, not covering my feeling that the whole thing was ridiculous, and said OK.

After the overnight at Ponil we packed up early and hiked out up South Ponil Canyon. They were headed for

the Baldy country and we would camp the night at
Pueblano. The way up the canyon bottom was easy and
we made camp before lunchtime. It felt good to be out
from under the packs before the heat of the afternoon
set in. We sprawled around in the shade of the pines and
lazed the hike fatigue away while we munched on the
lunch of crackers, peanut butter and jelly, and raisins.
The boys were rejuvenated after eating, and they went
off to join the hunter safety activity and shoot at the
running deer target on the 30-06 range. The leaders and I
were liking the afternoon's easy living, so we just let the
day run out while we loafed around camp. There was
plenty to talk about, and I enjoyed getting to know the
men. The boys would be late getting back from shooting,
so we interrupted our idleness long enough to get out
and gather in a supply of firewood for supper.

It was getting to be night before we got the meal done
and cleaned up. Then one of the boys got the guitar and
we settled in around the fire for a while. They were taking turns packing the instrument and were not having too
much trouble transporting it. Their only actual problem
was that after hauling it from Illinois to Pueblano, they
found that nobody knew how to play it. They were hoping
to get the hang of it on the trip. I took it and picked out
some camp songs. They sounded tinny and awful coming
out of the heavy painted, rusty-stringed box. I showed a
couple of the boys some chords and they said they'd
work on them. I wished I could hike on to Baldy with
this bunch, but my path for the next morning led straight
in the other direction, back down the canyon to get another group.

Within a week or so of my hike with the Illinois group I
picked up a crew from Ithaca, New York. After the first
morning's breakfast we got a bus to Ponil, a camp I was

beginning to feel pretty much at home in. We camped
there a night, then packed and unpacked and repacked
a couple of lop-eared burros and pulled their ornery
bodies over Hart's Peak to Indian Writings.

The leader was another Scout executive, and he and I
got to be good friends. He was a young field exec who
was just getting used to the frustrations built into his
business, ones like finding good volunteers to carry a
program and getting all the kids to act right most of the
time. Bob's wife was about to have a baby, and his mind
was on that a lot. Bob had worked a couple of college summers as a forest fire lookout, and he told me all about the
good life that it was, about living alone in a ranger hut
up in some really unpeopled wilderness, and scanning
from the lookout tower, and reporting in, and all. I took it
all in and filed the possibility away in my mind. It
sounded pretty near as good as rangering.

In the morning I hung around Indian Writings long
enough to walk along the canyon ledges and look at the
Indian petroglyphs, then hiked down the canyon to
where it ran into the main artery of the Ponil country.
Before long a dust cloud gusted up the canyon and a
yellow bus came rumbling ahead of it. It stopped and
took me in to headquarters, where I made the routine stop
at the Ranger office. Mr. Dunn said that one of my groups
had come by before leaving for home and had left something for me. He reached behind him and pulled out a
sadly weathered guitar. It had suffered multiple scratches,
and several nicks and dents in the wood showed where it
had met the trail. And on the back was an inscription and
the signatures of the whole Illinois group scrawled in felt
marker: "May your trail-weary bones outlive this trail-
weary guitar."

Another outing I remembered was with a bunch from

Paducah, Kentucky. I met them in a downpour one gray afternoon in headquarters. Their leaders were a couple of dads, one, a restaurant owner, and the other, Paducah's Chief of Police. The boys had heard a lot about the Tooth of Time and had seen the huge rock formation on the literature they had studied for the trip, so they wanted to take a firsthand look at the Tooth. Since the best way to do that was to camp right in front of it, they picked a route that started at Lovers' Leap Trail Camp.

The rain that had started when they rolled through Philmont's gateway was still going in a pattering, all-day drizzle on my wall tent in the morning. It was still going at its steady rhythm when we toted our packs to the loading dock, still coming down on us when the bus pulled away back toward headquarters and left us out on the trail to Lovers' Leap. Tooth of Time Ridge was invisible under the blanket of thick, low fog that had settled in on us. We hiked the mud road to a campsite and threw up a tarp to cover the packs while we went about setting tents out on the highest places we could find. The rest of the day we worked to get a decent bedding and a hot supper out of the soaked country and muddied waters we had been dumped in, and the ponchos we were living in soon were moist through to the inside. The wet logs had to be hacked open and the kindling whittled and pampered until a smoky fire was able to go by itself. The bedrolls at least stayed dry, and that was all to the good.

The new morning on the trail was as rainy as the day before, and its watery atmosphere was starting to get old. Moisture or mud had gotten to every article in the packs by now, and there would be no getting comfortable while rain was still coming down. We slogged through breakfast, then packed away the heavy, waterlogged tents and started up the mucky road toward Miners Park.

The Tooth was still soaring a half mile to the north, hidden behind a full, misty cloud. The Philmont trek was not turning out to be too much fun for the boys. Any of us would have bailed out, and there was not much to look forward to as long as the rainclouds hung there over all the countryside around us.

But halfway up the jeep trail to Miners Park, the cloud banks drifted apart and the drizzle slowed, then stopped. The boys came to life and whooped for joy when we hiked into camp, where a sunspray shone through the high fir and made the watery green plants glisten. We settled into one of the campsites that were scattered across the rich floor of the forest parkland and went about getting cleaned up. After lunch we got a fire going, and stick drying racks sprang up all around it. The restauranteur and the chief and I propped our boots up before the flames to dry, then spent the afternoon talking it over around the campfire and watching the steam roll off our hiking socks.

Not all of Philmont's appeal is owing to unusual happenings and adventures. Some of the satisfaction, if not most of it, is due just to living and being in its wilderness atmosphere. Such was especially the case concerning my intrigue with the Baldy country. For although nothing actually happened, the first junket I made through that area remains one of the most exhilarating and unforgettable experiences I have ever had. It was one of those things for which there was no obvious reason why it should have made such a dramatic and lasting impression. It just did. I had been hearing about the Baldy country all summer from Rangers who had made it back into those reaches of Philmont. Baldy was well known as

Philmont's tallest mountain, and I wanted to see it for myself. I got my chance right at the end of the summer, although I didn't expect to find anything much different from what I had already seen in other parts of the ranch.

I dropped my last trail crew of the summer at Dean Cow Camp. It was a Sunday, which is the only day you can tell apart from any of the others at Philmont, and that only by the visits of the chaplains, jeeping their way from camp to camp. I was especially eager to meet up with the chaplain on that particular Sunday, not out of any sudden religious thirst on my part, but due to a more secular desire for a ride to the Baldy country in his jeep; if I hiked the whole way up there, I wouldn't have any time to look around.

I bid the crew good-bye and good fortune, and took off on the trail that, before the day was over, would see me to the top of Baldy. My pack was riding light, and the winding jeep trail up and over Chandler Pass put up little resistance. As quickly as I made the Ponil Canyon road, a camp bus came along and carried me on into Ponil, where I hoped to make connections with a chaplain.

Ponil being a civilized camp, it was an easy matter to call headquarters and clear my jaunt with the Ranger office. Mr. Dunn gave me the next day off all right, and offered several words of advice and caution which were unnecessary but good to hear from someone who was in charge of a whole legion of ones like myself. I learned upon getting back to headquarters that the other Rangers who had left their groups that same day and hiked back into headquarters didn't get the usual following day off. Since camp was near closing, they had been put to work taking down Tent City. I'm sure I would have found myself rolling tents too, except that Mr. Dunn had this thing about wanting the Rangers to discover as much of Philmont as they could. "Men, *know* Philmont," he used to say.

Soon the Catholic priest finished his eight o'clock Mass, and we wedged my pack into the jeep's tight rear compartment and headed west up the South Ponil Canyon. The priest was no black-robed monk. He was, on the contrary, a lean and fit man with a face that reflected his youth and enthusiasm. He wore a Scouter's uniform, complete with shorts, knee socks, neckerchief, and a beret. His hand moved easily through the gearshift pattern, and his smooth downshifting on the inclines told that he was at ease on mountain trails. He made a friend of me immediately.

The canyon shone green, and a shallow stream rambled through its grassy floor, wandering across the jeep trail occasionally. We drove through Pueblano Camp and paused to talk with Scouts along the road there. Just out of Pueblano, we began to pass out of the frontal mountains and get into the real high country. The jeep rumbled up and around and over the rocky and eroded road. The jeep trail narrowed to a rough path between tall pines on both sides. The atmosphere became crisper and cooler, and its scent thinned to the single bracing fragrance of pine. The landscape was still and undisturbed by any evidence of civilization. We were into a land where men of Madison Avenue and Route 66 never go—a land of wilderness and man and suspended time. The trail led on for several long and thoroughly intriguing miles.

We wound our way up a final set of switchbacks and drove into Baldy Town Camp in time for lunch. The staff ran down to greet one of the few vehicles that would make its way to them all week. Father Fredette had mail for the staff, and that made them happy.

After eating I set out to explore the area. Baldy Town itself was perched on a knoll on the side of the huge Mount Baldy. Behind it the mountain soared abruptly, dense with a thick cover of the ranch's tallest Ponderosa pines. At the very top, above leveled shoulders on both sides, was the pink knob of the summit. All that was left of the old mining town there were the crumbling ruins of an old stone store and the brick chimney of the town's hotel. There were scattered foundations of cabins where the few hundred miners once lived. A really remarkable remnant of the town was the wooden piping of its water system. One section of the pipe was still usable, and brought water from the old reservoir that was just above the town site. Just below Baldy Town were the ruins of the Baldy Town gold mill. A couple of rusty tracks remained at the spot where gold ore was once fed into the plant. A dented, dirty-brown ore car lay by the tracks. Near the ore mill a couple of rusted car bodies of about 1930 vintage lay in a tall patch of weeds, wild flowers growing up through their broken windows. In the stream below, Scouts panned for gold dust.

The whole area reflected a sort of nostalgic paradox. The physical remains appeared to have lain undisturbed since the town's razing in the early forties. And while those ruins evidenced intensive activity in days past, the landscape around them was not that of a settlement shaped and cultivated by civilization. It was instead that of an isolated and untouched territory. Trees and plants grew as they wished. Giant timbers grew thick and full. This land was rich. I walked up an old mining road to the site of the Black Horse stamp mill. The road cut a groove around the side of the mountain, but its edges had become rounded off. It was grassed over, and saplings dotted its path. About a half mile from the site, the road became a trail that was rugged and narrow and considerably steep. And yet at its end was a thick and shady grove of trees in which stood the frame of what had been a substantial industrial unit. Still in place were rigid uprights that had once held the heavy stamp heads as they bludgeoned gold ore. Pine branches spread wide over the old foundation, and sizable trees now stood within inches of where the walls had once been. It remains to me a wonder how men equipped with the inferior vehicles and machinery available in those turn-of-the-century decades were able even to move all the materials and heavy equipment into the high reaches of the Baldy country, much less to install and maintain an industrial community in such an area. What strength there must have been in the lust for gold.

About the middle of the afternoon I started up the mountain. The whole area above Baldy Town was laced with overgrown mining roads. Along the trail were the entrances to long abandoned mine tunnels. A few had been boarded up some time ago, but others were open for a few feet to where the roof had caved in and the black, dank shaft was blocked by a wall of watery black debris. The mining road paths soon played out, and from there on, the best trail was the drainage bed up the saddle between the peak and its lower shoulder. The sketchy trail was a steep one, and the sun hardly penetrated the forest. A little stream ran down the narrow ravine that was sometimes the trail, and made it slippery.

It took far into the afternoon to get up the ravine. I was feeling like something of a buckskin man, having mountaineered my way from the mortal flatlands to one of the uppermost outstretched pinnacles of the earth. And then I came upon something that completely blew my mind. As the trail neared the top of the saddle, a small patch of sky appeared through the trees. Then all at once the trail emptied out into a vast grassy meadow that extended over the whole plateau-like top of the mountain shoulder. And moping around the meadow, munching on the grass and acting as though they thought they belonged there, was a herd—it looked more like a flock—of white-faced Hereford cattle. What a cow pasture was doing twelve thousand feet up and just below the commanding summit of Mount Baldy I don't know. Heidi and her grandfather couldn't have surprised me more.

Baldy's crowning hump was above the timberline and made a striking contrast to the rest of the mountain. It was of light-colored rock talus. The rocky fragments ranged from the size of a fist to several times that large. The rocks were loose and shifted beneath the weight of each step, so that scaling the last stretch to the top was a matter of scrambling up the unsteady rockslide hump. Old Baldy finally focused to a single plot that stood above the rest. Planted among the rocks of Baldy's top were the wind-tattered flags of Scout groups from places like Ohio and Massachusetts and New York. Their pride at having climbed the big one was inscribed on everything from handkerchiefs to towels and tied to sticks of every size.

Baldy's summit offers its own reward. I could have watched its wide panorama for days, but the falling sun would not allow it. I appreciated that moment as I have appreciated few others, sobered only by the realization that it could not last. The world of paint and asphalt and printed forms would claim me in a few days, and I was grateful for the interlude that this summer life had provided. There's a cold, hard rushing wind that blows high. That wind stirred my face while I looked upon the collage of green ridges and deep canyons below and beyond, and I knew that I would be coming back to this mountaintop world.

3

How far away was the summer world from the other one I had known. Two bus rides conveyed me between those two very different worlds. The routes to the high country and back to the Texas prairie and farmland were the same, year in and year out. Because the two ways of living were so different and because I had never ventured to familiarize myself with the territory that lay between them, the span between the mountain country and my home seemed far greater than the miles would have shown, the time away in the mountains far longer than the days would have shown. I only passed through whatever was between the two places in the space of a few night hours twice a year, sealed in the toxic highway capsule of a Greyhound bus.

When school finally let out and June rolled around, I would pack up everything I needed and take off for the summer. I set out for Philmont in a roundabout way, riding out across the hot, dry flats of West Texas to El Paso in the far western corner of the state. I rode through the midsized cities that had somehow rooted in at scattered places across the farmlands and oil fields, then the towns dwindled to a few as we rolled across miles and miles of the desolate sand hills and prairie brush to the city oasis of El Paso. There were sisters and cousins and an uncle and their families there, and they showed me some good times getting back to summertime things and taking in the border town.

Late in the afternoon of the day before I was supposed to be at Philmont, they took me downtown to the Greyhound station. I checked some baggage and bought myself a ticket for Raton, New Mexico. Just as the rush hour traffic began to filter into the busy street lanes, we boarded the musty, heavy-fumed coach and pulled out through the downtown streets, and I became a loner. The driver muscled the heavy coach onto a thoroughfare, and for long miles through the metropolitan layout I stared out the window at the hurried streets, the aging storefronts, the sprawling suburban shopping centers— the last I would see or feel of a real city for what seemed like a long, long time.

Suddenly the city was left behind and then Texas too was left behind, and there was only a narrow strip of pavement that lay straight ahead across the flat, barren expanse of sandy wasteland. I saw it out the window while we rode, facing out with a kind of hollow gaze. We rode for an hour or two and came to the desert town of Alamogordo, which sat out away from some low mountains to the east. We stopped at a station along the one main street that was also the highway. The same faded, weathered hamburger stand was always there across the street, and I walked over to buy a mangled hamburger with the money I had allowed for this segment of the trip. After supper we were back on the road. Once in a while I picked up a magazine or strange newspaper which I had bought to entertain me across the empty miles, but which somehow always ended up discarded in a dog-eared pile on the seat. Then for a long night we rode on and on and on in an uncomfortable half sleep, jangled into involuntary periods of consciousness for midnight stops at the stations in Albuquerque and Santa Fe. We cruised on over the face of New Mexico all through the night, and just at dawn pulled into the dark tunnel of a garage in Raton.

I straightened out my stiffened legs that had ridden scrooched up in a variety of awkward angles for so long, then got off the bus and strolled automatically out onto the street to breathe the light and cool early morning air that hinted of nearby mountains and of Colorado, only a few miles up the northern pass. I got my baggage together in one pile along the driveway's sidewalk, then went inside the crummy bus stop to sit among the magazine racks and the trinket cases and the pay toilets and the pinball machines, restless for full daylight and for the cafes to open.

There would always be a few other aimless ones waiting around, ones who bore some mark of men headed for Philmont, and we would soon go off to find some breakfast. The rest of the day was spent in periodic walks through town and through the shops and to the train depot, and back to dawdle at the bus stop. With every train and bus there would be a few more bound for Philmont, so that by the middle of the day groups of old friends and new ones roamed the streets together. By late afternoon there would be a mob of us, and four school buses and a high-walled truck would pull into a lot by the train depot and we would load up and be on our way across the forty-mile drive that brought us over a last stretch of plains and out to where the summer country began.

After a summer of being a Ranger I had had enough of headquarters. I wanted to work out in one of the mountain camps, to be at home up there with one place to sleep and eat, and a stable group of friends. My job was at Abreu Camp in the edge of the south country mountains. There were eight of us who loaded our gear onto a pickup and a panel wagon and made the first bumpy ride out across a dust-settled plain and up to the deserted clearing at the mouth of Rayado Canyon. There were a Camp Director, three rifle instructors, a commissary manager, a fly tying instructor, a conservation foreman, and me. It was my job to run an evening campfire telling the Philmont Story and also to show the first-day groups how to navigate the Philmont country with a map and compass.

The camp was situated in a place where Rayado Canyon's floor becomes broad as the river runs out of the mountains and rolls to the flat grasslands that start a mile down from camp. Abreu was peaceful in a way, set off from the rest of the ranch by the previous year's flood.

which had wiped out the nearby camps that would have held our neighbors. The flood had left other marks on Abreu, too. A floodplain flanked the little stream in a wide swath on either side and cut far into the washed-out banks. Strewn across the sand-filled bed of gravel and boulders were endless tangles of great pine logs. The camp's water system was ruined and the little pump house stood dormant for lack of new equipment. We took our drinking water straight from the river, and when it was muddy we would walk down to a little ravine where a spring ran clear all the time. The shower house was worthless, its buried steel guts ripped away by the flood. Upstream the river had cut a new channel around a ravaged island. The splintered boards of a latrine building lay flattened under a logjam in what had once been a campsite.

Our place was in a choppy little meadow bounded by mountains behind us, a low slate-crumbled hill across to the east, and the Rayado splashing down and away to the flatlands. The cabin sat just up from the riverbed in the edge of the meadow, facing down the canyon. Ed Wyatt issued trail food packets and sold a few items from a commissary-trading post that occupied the big room. The square little room that was left was where we cooked, ate, loafed, planned, and checked through to see what was happening. Up from the cabin was a row of four pale green wall tents where we slept.

There was always something going on in camp. The cabin was forever overcharged with the energy of so many active people darting around in so close a space. For mealtimes we wedged ourselves in around a picnic table and usually ended up in some lively discussion. In the daytime whenever we weren't working or eating, we found something else to be doing. If we didn't, John

Thompson would find something for us, because it was contrary to his principles to see anybody sitting idle while there was daylight. Most of the time we had our own chores to do. Every couple of weeks it would be time to take the washtub and scrubboard out back and wrestle clothes against them until the water quit turning muddy with each rinse.

At night we put on our campfire show in a spot up the meadow, then filled the cabin with coffee-drinking advisors. After they left we usually went on for another hour or two ourselves, plunking guitars or improvising some midnight treat or playing cards or just talking things over. One night a week we waited until the leaders left, then sat down to business around the table. There we ironed out the details of our operation and discussed matters among ourselves. We held forth for long hours when we got going on one of those sessions, and if we were ever going to come to blows over anything, we would do it there. When we were done nobody was in doubt about what we were trying to do or what was expected of him.

John Thompson was our leader from the first-day scrubdown and setting up to the last timbers we nailed in on the new bridge just before closing for the summer. John had just graduated from Clemson College and would take up his lieutenant's commission come September. His South Carolina upbringing came through in the flattest deep south drawl, especially when he wished we had some "ha-um and buttahbeans." John was not too tall, but he stood solid and came across hard and direct. He was a leader. He was constantly working at something, and he kept the rest of us that way too. John was at the middle of the action, whether it was fun or work. But when he got down to serious business, his dark eyes came set to a piercing stare and he spoke from a stern, angular jaw that decided things with a definite finality. To John there was a right way to do everything, and nothing less would do for Abreu. John believed in doing his job right, and he expected the same of each of us. He got it.

The Camp Director believed in putting in a day's work whether there was any to be done or not, so we became a staff of builders. There was enough of the old black plastic pipe from the water system that some of the boys were able to hook up a gravity flow water pipe by wedging one end between rocks at a high place about a half mile up the river. From there they ran the pipe down the dry channel of the floodplain to a gully behind the cabin. There it ran into an old steel stock tank that we had found and moved in there. The tank was a round, corrugated steel vat about ten feet across and waist-deep. It became our swimming pool. Before long Terry Dunn had added an aquatic safety rack with rescue pole and life ring. The life ring was sawed from some old two-by-six studs and was wrapped with tape and cloth, then painted and garnished with the proper rope handles. If it had ever been thrown to a swimmer, it would probably have killed him instantly.

John was good at seeing things for us to do at Abreu. We cleared out brush and developed new campsites to make up for the ones ruined in the flood. We dragged new logs up from the stream to the campfire and cut and trimmed them and set them in to replace the rotting ones being used for seats. We rocked in the area around the cabin where runoff from the roof had washed dirt out from around the foundation. Dick Schlaeppi was the fly tying man, and he spent the better part of the summer building a log fly tying shelter with the help of others from time to time. There was no shortage of logs there on a bank above the stream. Dick would take his ax over nearly every day to cut and notch the logs to a fit, and the adirondack took shape and was finished before the summer was.

We were never satisfied with the flimsy footbridge that had been thrown across the Rayado just after the flood. The one other thing we had to do before the summer ended was to build one that would stay. Todd had his conservation boys out cutting cross logs for a week or two, while the ones engineering the project searched through the logjams for the two biggest ones to lay across the river. On a day when we had plenty of groups in camp, we got the campers up to where the main logs were and moved the logs down to the bridge site. We used several of the cross logs to support the big ones, which were a good fifty feet or so in length and a couple of feet in diameter. With sixty or eighty boys around the logs, we inched them down to the place. The afternoon gave into a true spectacle. It reminded me of one of those cast-of-thousands movies—Egyptian slave masses building the pyramids or something. We rocked in foundations on both banks, then worked the logs across and laid them in place and leveled them. When the box of eight-inch nails came in, we finished by hammering down the cross logs. The old plank bridge was dinky beside the new one, which would have accommodated a Mack truck.

Around camp the days were all alike. They rolled on in a sameness broken only by the treks that we each made out into the civilized world every two weeks. At Abreu there was nothing much of importance about the particular day of the week or month. There was nothing liberating about Friday afternoon, nothing casual about Saturday, nothing dismal about Monday morning. More often than not, we didn't know what day it was and didn't care. Each was just one more day when new Scout groups would hike into camp and take part in our regular activities. Every day brought its share of adventures and interesting characters, but there was no kind of routine tied to the calendar.

There was one day, though, that we could anchor to for some sense of time, one day that had something of its own to distinguish itself from the others. That day was Sunday. We were on the chaplain's circuit, and we came to look forward to his weekly visits and to the short Sunday gatherings we had in the evening. Of the eight of us at Abreu, four of us discovered that we had an insurmountable majority over the others in church affiliation. So just to make something of it, we created a militant cheer on behalf of Methodism. When Sunday morning came around, then, we would stand together around the breakfast table and yell it through the roof to inaugurate the day.

Sometime after supper the chaplain's jeep would purr from down the canyon, and we would run out to leap on any mail that he might be bringing when he rounded the last bend and came into the clearing. Pretty soon the groups trickled in from the various outer campsites, and we took the chaplain's religion box and led them up a winding path to a flat opening at the top edge of the eastern hill. There we had a kind of chapel area with some log seats and an altar of stacked rock, and at the point of the hill stood a rough-hacked cross jutting above the valley. If the reverend had never spoken a word, it would still have been worth it to sit up on that little plot and look down over our camp and out across the tree-covered slopes of Rayado Canyon. We could see beyond to the far peaks and gaze along the distant soaring crest of the rimrock. While the last sinking rays of hazy sunlight tinted the westward slopes and shadows deepened in the low-lying hollows, we could not but feel something. There was nothing particularly devout or religious about any of us, but we appreciated that one quiet time each week when we sat on a hilltop to look out over it all. The great doctor used to talk about "reverence for life," and maybe that is what we felt.

The groups liked being in Abreu and we liked having it that way. They were at Philmont to have a time they would never want to forget, and we got in the habit of trying to see that they had it. We anticipated times when a little thinking on our part could make a difference in how things were going for them. Whenever it rained, the stream was going to be muddy; so if it looked like rain was coming we would get out all the buckets we had and fill them out of the river while it still ran clear and line them up on the porch, so that there would be some good water for cooking and drinking when the groups came in. We kept a supply of dry wood stashed out in the pump house for those days and rationed it out to them. If any of the boys had wet sleeping bags, we would get the wet bedding and drape it across the cabin rafters, because we had all been acquainted with the miserable and demoralizing experience of sleeping wet. We made friends among the groups where we could and made a point of speaking to the kids we would see around camp, and often enough some boy or leader or some incident would seem to make that effort worthwhile.

One feature of a Philmont expedition is the chance to meet other Scouts from all over the country as you traverse the mountains. Philmont brings together groups from every state and from the U.S. territories, and sometimes from foreign lands. But out there on the trails it is hard to find a stranger. There are no walls to separate people, and it is easy to walk into a new bunch and know them pretty well right off.

The national-international flavor that is created gets into the whole trip and is something that the boys are aware of and look for as they go along. If there is one thing that all of the groups have in common, it is a pride in their own home states. The boys find plenty of ways to express the regional spirit that they and their friends share across the miles. Every city group that passes through a settled camp will want to know how their Cards or Braves or Red Sox are doing. Some groups hike in uniform hats or T-shirts that show where they are from. Others may carry a supply of small souvenirs from a local feature or well-known industry and give them to friends made along the way.

Some of the boys, though, seem to delight in inciting friendly rivalries between regions, and none of them mind participating. It seems, for example, to be regarded as an extreme breach of conduct for North Carolina boys to venture out of the old South without carrying a Confederate flag. It may be, and I think this is the case, that they have a mortal fear of being taken for Yankees, an unlikely prospect given their always droll accent and their usually extreme penchant for vocalizing it. At any rate, it seems to be a rule. It is as though General Lee would yet cringe in his grave if the Stars and Bars were ever left behind. At any given moment a Rebel flag may appear along the trail, at a chapel gathering, or even in the john.

One place where regional fervor runs high is at the evening campfire programs. Then and there the boys can get down to some fun with the songs and stories and general foolishness that will come unraveled as the night gets along. Once in a while there will be a group that is pretty impressed with its local characteristics, and sometimes there will be those to differ with them. Although the original scrap is well into history by now, the old Civil War grudge is still good for an argument when there are groups around from both regions. We always hated for that to come up, because at Abreu the southern boys came out on the short end of most North-South confrontations. Out of the eight on the staff, only three of us were southern, including the Camp Director, who was pretty much immune to the hostility of the others. This left just two of the younger ones, Ed Wyatt and me, to defend old Dixie, a duty we never wanted, but something that seemed rather expected of us. Ed and I both were Texans, which made it doubly bad on us, and more than once we came close to getting thrown in the Rayado River for that heinous flaw. People from the United States are very sensitive on the subject of Texas. All one has to do in order to be labeled a braggart in Yankeeland is to indicate that he resides within the boundaries of Texas.

One evening along in the summer Abreu turned Texan when four or five Texas crews turned out to be our population for the night. Ed and I were delighted to be among our folks for once, and we wasted no time in picking up on it. We were in a high mood when we struck up the evening's campfire, and as the night wore on, it took on a distinctly Texan flavor. We opened with "The Eyes of Texas," closed with it, and threw it in parenthetically several times. The sound of it soon wore thin on our un-Texan staff friends, and they said so, which but stoked the fire. Kids who would never have opened their mouths to sing at home were happily yelling themselves hoarse over "The Eyes of Texas," singing it out for the benefit of those present who didn't want to hear it. We had what you might call a good old time.

Maybe Ed and I would not have pushed the Texas stuff quite so far if we had been thinking ahead a little to when we would be on our own again. In the morning we were out early to see our Texas boys on their way, and we had a good feeling of satisfaction in seeing them hike out over the hill to the tune of "The Eyes." Our delight, however, soon turned to dismay. Soon after the Texans all had left, a crew from Ohio hiked in, then another, and another. More came in the afternoon, and by nightfall Abreu was crawling with those rascals. Two of our staff friends were from Ohio, and they set about to organize.

When dusk fell we walked up for the campfire, Ed and John and I feeling somewhat the outsiders among sixty loud Yankees. We just minded our own business and hoped that nothing would ever come of it, but that was too much to expect. Our five mates from the Abreu staff could not pass up the chance to do old Dixie in. Wisecracks flowed and we just sat there like three rocks. Since the Ohioans didn't have anything to brag about in their state, they took up taunting us about the Union winning some war a long time ago. We didn't care too much about that, but they began to come out with a bunch of low expressions against the Southland. Then they even set in to badmouth Texas. The Rebs didn't say anything.

We went ahead into the Philmont Story, and then concluded with the Philmont Hymn. The Scouts sobered up for one serious moment and stared into the fire's red embers while the notes faded into an inspirational-type silence. Proud strains of "Dixie" broke the night air from the back row. The Ohio mob set upon John and Ed with visions of them floundering in the river. I was fixing to put out the fire when I chanced to look up and see a rather large pile-up on top of my brothers. I took my bucket of water and stood in the darkest shadow of a big pine tree and bellowed, "Oh, I wish I was in the land of Cotton. Old times there are not forgotten. Look away . . ."

"Get 'im!" somebody yelled, and the mob dropped John and Ed, and came after me to end the sacrilege. As they came in close I let the bucket fly and flung water all over as many of those damned Yankees as I could hit. I delighted in their shrieks and oaths. A bunch of them laid into me, thinking to immerse my body in the Rayado. They thought wrong. I kicked and fought and flailed away, causing one of the Ohio staff guys to warn his ruffians, "Watch out for his legs; He's got track legs." Two more Yankees came up to help them handle me, but the Ohio boys thought they were John and Ed there in the dark and jumped them, giving forth with some unscoutlike words. I kept kicking and bolting and raring, and finally I came loose. While the confusion went on, I used my track legs to get me down to the cabin, where John and Ed were waiting, John standing on the porch facing up the draw with the barrel of a broom across his arm.

We had a good laugh at our outsmarting sixty Yankees, and then got on with serving coffee to the Scout leaders. Before long the Ohio campers passed the cabin going back to their tent sites, and the staff Yanks came dragging in the door. They were all ruffled and dirty. One held a handkerchief to his bloody nose and wore a long rip in his shirt. All of them were scratched up and their clothes were trashed beyond repair. They told how the Ohio kids had rassled them down toward the creek for fifteen minutes thinking sure that they were John and Ed and I. One of them remarked that he was sorry to get beat up, but was glad to know that his fellow Ohioans had the right idea about southerners.

Philmont, as well as being a national Scout camp, operates as a working ranch, running upward of five hundred head of prime Hereford cattle. Abreu was right in the middle of the cow country, and the grass of Abreu must have been very sweet, because some of those cattle kept it cut short for us all summer.

A frequent visitor to Abreu was the cattle department foreman, "Booger" Brown. Booger was a western cowboy if there ever was one. He was pretty short and walked bowlegged. He chewed tobacco and spat the juice wherever he pleased. He was missing about half his teeth, as one could easily tell by the way he talked. His conversation was spiced with cuss words and he didn't follow all the rules of English grammar, but he could sure express himself. Booger was very friendly and likable, and all of the camp staffs were glad to see him come riding in, and to offer him a cup of coffee and a sandwich.

Booger was right at home in the south country camps. He had the habit of taking a nap after lunch every day wherever he might be working, so, like the proverbial sailor with a girl in every port, Booger had a bed in every camp. Anyone who had been around Philmont for a while could walk into the cabin at a camp and see a cot with just a mattress on it sitting in the corner and would know right away that it was "Booger's bed."

It was a lot of fun just to sit around and watch Booger lie and cuss and spit on the floor. It was a treat whenever Booger came up to Abreu. He never came into camp without trying to instigate a move to throw the Camp Director in the Rayado.

Booger was an avid horseshoe player. We had a lot of good games with our two stakes and four old rusty shoes of different sizes. We always got a session going when Booger was in camp, and he rarely lost a game. He had a peculiar lopsided style, but it worked. He would squat down a little and give the shoe a kind of sidearm motion that made it go wobbling out through the air, revolving as it went. He had a couple of expressions he would use whenever a play didn't go his way. He had a mild oath for a poor throw of his own, and whenever the opposing team made a ringer, he would come out with a little saltier term. By Booger's rules a legitimate part of the game was trying to rattle the other team, so just when you were ready to release a throw with intense concentration, Booger would make a bowlegged leap into the air yelling "Look out, Red!" We would practice hard when we knew Booger was coming, the horseshoe player's highest ambition being to beat Booger.

Nobody at Abreu drank coffee, but we kept a pot on the stove for the Scout leaders. Since none of us drank it, we would make our boiled coffee, adding more water and more grounds until the pot was full of grounds, about two weeks to the pot. Leaders would make chiding comments about the taste of our coffee, but we never thought much about it until Booger was up one day. Booger liked strong coffee, so when he took a mouthful of ours and spewed it out all over the porch and hollered "Make some more!" we knew it was time to change grounds.

The downpour had slackened, but a drawn-out drizzling spell hung over Abreu. The thick mist fogged Rayado Canyon while widening puddles made the ground sloppier by the hour. We huddled around the kitchen table whenever there weren't groups to handle and tried to look busy when there were. We were sitting out the afternoon until two Scouts ran into camp and gasped out something about a boy with a broken foot. We got them out of their muddy ponchos and slowed them down, then asked what we needed to know. Their group had been hiking down the canyon from Fish Camp when one of them lost his balance crossing the stream and fell hard against his ankle. The ankle was broken. The boy was running a fever and the foot was swollen; he couldn't stand on it. The group was stopped along the trail at the campsite near the Rayado Crags and would wait there until help came. And another thing, they cautioned us, the fallen boy was a hefty one, around three hundred pounds.

A boy with a broken foot would not be walking out of Rayado Canyon in a rainstorm. It was not all that easy a hike under the best of conditions. Bill got on the C.B. unit and contacted the Health Lodge in headquarters. There was no road near the Crags area and the road into Fish Camp had been made treacherous by the flood. In the rainy weather it would be impassable. The boy would have to be carried down to Abreu and taken in from there. There was no work to be done on the rifle range in the rain, so two of the shooting instructors took down the steel-frame basket stretcher and went off up the canyon. They had never hiked Rayado Canyon and were not at all certain where the Crags camp was. Neither was anybody else.

When the stretcher carriers had left, we had time to radio headquarters the name and group of the injured boy, and to let them know that we had help on the way. A vehicle would be ready to come out for the boy as soon as we had him in camp. An hour passed and there was no word from the Crags. Two hours, still nothing. After three hours it was nearly dark, and there was still no sign of the stretcher crew. Something had gone wrong or the rain had just slowed them to a crawl. Either way, they would need some help. Dick Schlaeppi and I pulled ponchos over our heads and grabbed a flashlight. Headquarters could not tell us much more about the location of the trail camp at the Crags than we already knew, but the canyon was a deep and narrow one, and if there were people camped in it, we would find them.

We hit a quick step up the canyon road, and about a half mile up, just below the Abreu hunting lodge, we met the original rescuers returning. Their faces were drawn and muddy, their step was labored, their stretcher was empty. They swore to having covered the next three or four miles of canyon, finding no trace of people, and the Crags camp was supposed to be no more than three miles above Abreu. Dick and I interrogated them at length and satisfied ourselves that they had been fooled by the ruggedness of the terrain into thinking they had come farther than they actually had. We took the stretcher from them and lunged ahead up the darkening canyon. We passed the hunting lodge, and, with it, left the good broad road behind.

We searched behind the lodge and found the wisp of a trail disappearing to the west. The trail zigzagged up and down the steep slope of the canyon, just above a bluff where the incline dropped nearly straight down to the river. The path was slick, its wet face more like ice than like conventional mud. It was not deep-soaked and squishy, but instead was covered with a film of fine clay mud, then stony hard underneath. We slid down often and could not have made the trail at all except for the trees alongside it that we could grab onto. An off-and-on drizzle kept the trail slippery, and we crept along making maybe a mile an hour. The trail wound down the canyon side and opened onto a broad floodplain where Bonito Canyon merged into the Rayado. We took the Rayado way and followed the trail across the river and into a heavy, dark undergrowth of scrub oak and pine saplings under a taller stand of fir timbers. Darkness was setting in, and we could only follow the trail by looking for lighter gaps where we could see between the trees and fallen logs.

If a man had wanted to get himself really lost, really isolated in the most uncharted and unreachable depths of the Philmont wilds, he could not have chosen a more likely area than the upper reaches of Rayado Canyon. Between the high-pitched walls of Rimrock Mesa and Philmont's southern peaks was the deep gorge through which coursed the chilly Rayado. There were no roads, no outposts, no meadows. Rayado Canyon had taken the worst of the destruction dished out by the flood a year before. The fine log buildings of Waite Phillips' Fish Camp retreat had been battered, the kitchen of the main lodge ripped off and hurled down the stream torrent. Bits of it could still be found down the miles of canyon, and we stumbled across a couple of them as we made our way along. Olympia Camp, farther down the canyon, had been left in a graveled floodplain, useless for camping.

Endless miles of logjams and boulder train reminded of the force of the waters that had gouged ragged scars out of the countryside. Whole sections of the canyonsides had been swept down the river. The trail was there only in short overgrown stretches that had to be hunted for and might lead to the edge of a little cliff or overhang. The canyon walls in some places dropped off almost straight down to the water. Boulders and logjams clogged the whole river bottom, making it impractical to follow the path of the streambed. The stretch from Abreu to Fish Camp had always been one of the hardest hikes, but after the flood it was a long obstacle course requiring countless dozens of stream crossings in the space of its six miles.

By the time we had gone a half mile past the fork, we were sweating enough inside the ponchos that the drizzle could get us no wetter. We stopped to shuck the raincoats and put them in the stretcher. At the same time we gave in to darkness and began using the flashlight. The trail, where we could find it, only got worse as we went along. Neither Dick nor I had ever been this way, and the farther we ventured, the more sensitive we became to the growing black expanse of badlands we were putting between us and our camp, an expanse over which we were not sure we could retrace our path. We crept farther into the black unknown. We alternated between trying to walk along the bank above the river and down in the streambed itself. Neither was fit for hiking, but as one would become impassable we would switch to the other, always hoping for a good long stretch with smooth grass and no rocks.

We trudged up the canyon for another couple of hours, calling to the group and looking for flames in the dark wood. We spoke of turning back now and then, but were hung up on the thought that the group would be just around the river's next bend. On the wooded shelf above the streambed we would once in a while run onto a segment of reasonable trail, only to have it lead into a thicket where we would bump and turn and poke around for the path, then give it up once again. Sometimes the riverbed would offer a few hundred yards of soft gravel flats, but these would inevitably become, at the river's next turn, heaps of boulders too time-consuming to scale and to rugged to scramble around.

The night wore long and we began hearing voices that

weren't there. We would see the flames of a distant camp-fire, then see that when the clouds had drifted apart briefly, we were only looking at moonlight reflected off a wet boulder. The flashlight's power waned, though we tried to save it for only the worst places, and finally it dimmed to a dull glow. The rain would start up once in a while, soaking through our clinging, drippy shirts and running off our heads and down under our clothes. If we had not been keeping busy, it would have been miserable —in fact, it was anyway.

We dropped the stretcher and sat down to consider the situation for the hundredth time. We swelled our lungs and yelled into the canyon as far as our voices would carry. There was no answer. We surely had passed the Crags by now, so the campers had to have made their way back up to Fish Camp. At a little before midnight we gave up the hunt. We sat in the gravel plain a little longer looking up at the narrow skyway above the tall black walls of the canyon slit. We looked at the puny flashlight and thought of the tedious way back and of the hard, rocky passes whose number we could no longer quite remember. We felt the bruises and scratches all over us and thought of the comfortable cot beds that were gruesome hours away. The stretcher was getting to be an albatross, but we had to get it home. We picked it up and started back. The flashlight faded to a reddened filament, then went dead. When the light was gone we stuck to the streambed as much as we could, wading right down the frigid chan-nel some of the time. While the upper bank was steep, dark, and strewn with downed timbers, the riverbed's main drawback was the sea of awkward boulders that lined its length. There was but little sand and gravel-fill among the big rocks to make the walking any easier. Dick was leading the way now, and I followed in a stupor at the back of the stretcher. Gradually we unwound our complicated trail, dragging our feet over, around, and into rock after rock after rock. For two hours we pulled each other over those boulders before we regained the Bonito Canyon fork.

We relaxed a little after finding the fork. There were still two bad miles ahead of us, but at least we had a trail, however slick, to see us the rest of the way. We wanted to ditch the stretcher and come back for it at some more pleasant occasion, but we ended up carrying it on. The winding part back to the hunting lodge was more slippery than before, and we spent most of that stretch sliding down against the wet, crumbling bark of trail-side trees and picking ourselves back up again. The trail was up among the timbers and harder to follow in the midnight darkness. We could only find our way by feeling the slickness of bare mud against rocky slope on the up and down sides. Gully washes cutting down across the slope faked us off the trail, and finally we lost it entirely. We bushwhacked through the underbrush on a bluff above the river which we could hear gurgling across the little rapids below. We ran aground on a water pipe and followed it to a steel tank. Behind it were the stark outlines of the old barn and the stout, angled hunting lodge against the clouded sky. We hurried and crossed the bridge to the service road. Though we sunk into its softened mudbed, the wide road had a welcome feeling after the untamed route we had followed. It moved easily under feet that had become more accustomed to groping and climbing than walking.

We walked into Abreu and left the stretcher on the long porch. The camp, even in the smallest morning hours, was a friendly place. There were good tents and dry bedding and the paths were all where they were supposed to be. Dick and I got a couple of buckets and stripped down by the water faucet to wash the mud from our arms and legs. We scrubbed the dried-up cuts and exchanged a few words about where we had been. We wondered once more where the crippled boy was, then headed up to the dry flannel bedrolls.

I got up about the middle of the morning and limped down to the cabin, where I spent most of the day in a rocking chair on the porch. The morning had brought no news on the injured boy, and headquarters was about to send a rescue party up to Fish Camp. Then, about noon, the lost group came hiking down the road and into camp. At the rear was the boy hippo himself, skipping along on his "broken" foot and carrying a walking stick for effect. His lousy foot wasn't even swollen. Dick and I walked around him and wondered what had ever made us think we could get him down Rayado Canyon in a stretcher.

Dick and I talked to some of the boys in the group and mentioned how we had spent the previous evening looking for them. The campers got the others and told them to come up and have a look at me. The Scouts scanned me up and down and sized up the collage of bruises and scabs that mottled my arms and legs. They examined me with great curiosity and weighed the situation, then declared that my condition was twice as critical as the foot patient's had ever been.

There was no single day of abandonment at the end of the summer comparable to the opening-day mob scene. Rather, the staff men and camping groups dwindled away daily over the last two or three weeks until none were left but the few who lived there. Daily increments of Rangers were turned loose around the twentieth of August. Following that the mountain camps were closed out a few at a time as the last expeditions moved through them and went on. Last to go, on the final day, were the ones who kept headquarters open—the people who worked the food lines, the trading post, the Tent City offices.

Packing up all of the stuff that I had brought out and that had accumulated over the course of the summer, and then wrangling it through a day of bus transfers, was a tedious prospect—and one that I didn't really like. Still, I found myself looking forward to a few easy days at home before school started up. When I got around to pulling the dusty footlocker out from under my cot and went to repack everything for the trip home, I invariably found that my belongings would not anywhere near fit into the assortment of bags I had brought out. With that discovery began a game of spacial efficiency. First there would be at least one, and more often two or three, pairs of shoes and hike boots that were done in beyond repair. Those could go in the nearest trash can or be tied together and slung up over the gateway to hang with a dozen other pairs that had done the trail. From then on it was just a matter of fitting everything in at the proper angle and making sure no space went unused. I took meticulous care in that, even to the point of throwing away the worn-out batteries from my flashlight and stuffing two or three socks into the empty barrel.

There was one annoying obstacle to deal with—I always managed somehow to have to lug home both a banjo and a guitar, whether I had taken them both out to New Mexico with me or not. Baggage processing has never done too much good for the musical quality and general longevity of instruments, so it was not easy to get them home in one piece. The guitars that I had never represented much of an investment, so those I just checked through the baggage line—that is after loosening the strings and stuffing the sound box full of dirty clothes, then strapping the lid down over the case with an old web belt.

The banjo was more complicated. I had no case for it, so about the closest I could come to protecting it from the wear and tear it was bound to get was to sandwich it in between some clothes hanging in a suit bag. This left the peghead and the long, thin neck sticking far out at the top, so those I padded by pulling a couple of the long Scout knee socks down over the neck and tucking them into the clothes bag. Then I carried the whole thing with me for the entire trip—on the bus, at station stops, to the rest rooms. The lumpy suit bag with a green sock sticking out of it went where I went.

Getting from the mountain country over to a main highway, then into Texas, down across the Panhandle, and to Abilene took up what amounted to one long day with a night stuck in the middle of it. When it was over I would find myself back among the places and people and habits that were familiar from a young lifetime. And then the summer life would be something far away and gone entirely, but for futile attempts to bring it to mind in daydreams that could not quite cut through the sultry days and hot winds of the Texas plains.

Once or twice a day the ranch ran one of the school buses into Raton to take the leaving ones to their trains and buses. Then there would be another day of waiting and wandering until the eastbound Greyhound came through Raton in late afternoon. Finally our baggage was checked through, and we pulled onto the road and off over the straight highway ribbon that crossed the plain toward Clayton. The town, the cutoff to Cimarron, the low ripple of mountains in the sunset were left to fade and recede until finally they were too far back to matter.

After a few minutes' stop at some nameless roadside greasy spoon we rolled on over the plains and crossed the state line, and the extra hour of time that had been so freely given at the beginning of the summer was jerked away. Like any other native Texan who has fully taken on the Texas feeling of nationality, I somehow felt better and safer to be back in Texas. There was, of course, no sense to that feeling; it came on me not because there was anything lacking about New Mexico or anything better about this point along a highway than the ones behind it, but just because this was Texas. I started to notice the countryside and to look out at the roadside that had previously been passing before an indifferent gaze. Whatever else this land was or wasn't, at least it was Texas.

We rolled on across the flatland and the long twilight evening wore into night. The summer was over. This night always found me beside the bus window, bounded by the strong highway whirr of the heavy Greyhound engine and the dull lights along the aisle, gazing out at the star specks and at the passing headlights, caught in a reflective mood that lasted long into the night and down across the Panhandle into the more familiar parts of West Texas. After a last midnight rest stop I dozed across the late miles until we cruised around Sweetwater and came into well-known territory. There I came awake and looked out at what I could see of the dark home country.

We bore down the wide double stripe of Highway 80, more recently I-20, and soon there were the lights of Abilene spread in a low fan across the plain. We rolled straight on up South First beside the railroad, and I stirred to get my stuff together. I eased up the aisle past the head-drooping sleepers and crouched beside the driver and pointed at a traffic light up ahead where I wanted to get off. The coach ground against its own weighty momentum and came to stop at the red light, and I stepped off into the warm night of home, still lugging along the banjo suit bag.

While the bus pulled away toward downtown I stood long enough to shuck the jacket I had worn from the cooler New Mexico elevation, then walked away down Sayles Boulevard with a sidewalk passing somewhat strangely under the muscular stride that had not quite stopped hiking. I walked down the comfortable boulevard that had been the way to town forever, down the wide street of broadleaf shade trees and the big homes where Abilene's leading citizens lived, or had once lived. High arching streetlights shone a soft glow on the walks and houses. The long street was still and peaceful, and undisturbed except for me and an occasional slow-moving auto. I continued down across South Seventh, past the long, half-hidden mansion that we knew vaguely as the "Jones Estate," past the Jay home, past the corner house with the low rock fence, past the house where the bird dogs barked when our daddy used to take us walking.

At my music teacher's brick home I turned off the boulevard, the eastern sky turning light behind me, and walked toward home, down the long hill toward the gray painted house on Grand Avenue, and finally into my backyard. There I stopped, just to look at the garbage cans and the roof-line and the pecan tree and the air conditioner and the garage and all of those things that were so personal and that had seemed so far away. Already the earth was warm and the air was steeped in a dry heat, and the sun was impatient to come up over Dr. McFadden's big, two-story house. It was going to be a scorcher. I set the rumpled banjo bundle down while I fumbled for my door key, then jiggled it in the tumbler, and the wandering boy came home.

4

At Ponil we were not exactly tucked away in a high mountain cove. Ponil was the big central camp of the north country, and it stood a heavy daily barrage of camping groups and service traffic. Ponil is a sprawling sort of camp that covers more than two miles of the wide, flat bottom of Ponil Canyon. It sits in a low open space once called Five Points for the five canyons that converge there; it is, in fact, the locus of trails dispersed to the whole north country.

The north country is a land pretty much to itself. It is divided from the southern parts by the asphalt scar of U.S. 64 running the length of Cimarron Canyon. The north has its own character. Except for the verdant Baldy region, the north country mountains lie in gathered folds of canyons and brown-shaded ridges that are more sparsely timbered than the south. The free-flowing crystal waters that trickle through the southern mountains are hard to come by farther north, where water is a precious commodity culled from a few scattered springs and wells.

Those northern reaches, though, are crusty with relics that have silently decayed. The Indian writings, some excavated prehistoric dwellings, the fading overgrown bed of the loggers' line, the ruins of a logging camp, Black Jack Ketchum's outlaw hideout, and the Baldy mining region all are to be found strewn over the hard and foreboding north. The northern mountains are very much apart from the green south and its pattern of backcountry camps scattered through the mountains in a great rugged fan from headquarters. Ponil was at the middle of the rough northern lobe of Philmont, and except for a seldom used back road into the Baldy region, the way into the north country was through Ponil.

Ponil Canyon was a long valley that converged in three forks to wind its way down through the miles of mountain ranchland and out to the eastern plain. A dirt road followed the canyon floor to bring vehicles over the twelve-mile course from the Raton highway and from headquarters to our sprawling backwoods settlement. Just below camp was the long pasture where the horses ran loose between rides. At the lower end of Ponil were the horse barns with their bunkhouse and high-walled corrals where the three wranglers worked at getting the boys saddled up for rides and showing groups how to go about saddling and packing their burros. Just beyond was the fenced acre where fifty to a hundred burros switched their tails and stood in dumb clusters around the few shade trees, and across the road were the permanent log homes of Fred, the horseman, and Max, the maintenance man.

Further up, the canyon floor spread wider, and the stout log buildings left from the Philturn era were scattered along the next half mile. There were a dining lodge, the commissary, a small office cubicle, the "Long House," and our staff cabin which lay across a narrow suspension foot-bridge and against the ridge. Beyond those stretched a mile or two of the scattered troop campsites, including the suburb camps of Sioux and Bent.

Ponil was a fast-moving place, and it often took all that we had to keep up with it. We rarely camped fewer than a hundred Scouts a night and sometimes had over two hundred. There were maintenance men and supply trucks coming through most days, and several times each day the yellow buses rumbled in to turn new starting groups out into the north country. It was hard to make Ponil anything more than an easy stopover and a service depot for the more isolated camps, but Dave Shumway was the Camp Director, and he was determined that Ponil would be a Scout camp too. Dave was a medical student who had done a lot of scouting in Iowa, but he was doing his first summer at Philmont and was set on fulfilling a respon-sibility to the kids who might be looking forward to Ponil.

Besides Dave and the permanent men and the wran-glers, there were a cook named Kermit, a commissary man, a quartermaster, a trading post manager, and two moun-taineering instructors. I was responsible for the evening program and was Dave's assistant director, which took in a lot of things. My main chore was doing things for people. Most of my time was spent in walking up and down the canyon to show groups into a campsite or to check them out. The rest of the day I handled the miscellaneous problems and situations that leaders would always be coming in with. Then there were some conservation presentations that we were responsible collectively for giving to the first-day groups, and I usually ended up with those, often at odd hours. Dave was hung up on working with the groups at their convenience—running the camp for the Scouts—so if somebody wanted to talk about conservation before breakfast or late at night, that is what I would be doing then.

Ponil's days were long and harrowing, but I would still have been glad for a few more of them. At the crack of dawn an alarm clock detonated from a table in the middle room where we had set it to give it a fair chance of getting us up. The four of us who lived in the far cabin pulled on some clothes and stumbled off across the bridge and down the road toward the dining hall before the sun had even begun to come over Hart's Peak. Before we could get down to the dining lodge, Kermit would usually step out onto the back porch, resplendent in his white, full-length kitchen apron, and pull a few clangs off on the dinner bell. The main hall of the big log lodge was almost dark except for a couple of evening hours when the generator ran, and the place rattled with the dozen of us eating at two tables in a place built for seventy or eighty.

After breakfast we went to work on our various jobs. For me that meant heading back to the office cabin to stand ready for the dozens of small errands that would fill the day. The office was dark and cool, cavelike beneath the bank of tall cottonwoods, so I spent the first hour loitering in the sunshine out by the flagpole. Soon groups began checking in and out and people started needing things, and we would quickly be caught up in a hurried day. Between chores I would get back to the office, and if the lag was very long, Dave and I would take stock of our operation and debate ideas that we had about how things should be. Dave had come stubbornly intent on running a very top camp, and we spent hours mulling over the various aspects of its staff and program and everything.

Ponil kept me busy. Though there was no preset routine of work every day, it happened that as soon as we would get one thing taken care of, there were one or two new things that had to be done. Lots of times the day's groups would come in on top of each other and keep us running until we could get away for some lunch in the middle of the afternoon. I had never worked any harder before Ponil, but the job was made up of miscellany. I could go straight through a day from before breakfast until late at night just staying above water, then not be able to recall any particular thing I had done when walking across the dark canyon to bed and telling myself what a hard day it had been.

Since Ponil was one of the two sprawling base camps on Philmont, it would have been easy for us to have been overwhelmed by the mobs of Scout groups that came through every day. We could have put in a pretty full summer without ever getting to know any of the people who were passing through. But fortunately we didn't let that happen, and it paid us something in meeting some unforgettable men. One was a gruff old bear who ran a troop in the Loop area of Chicago—gangland. The four or five boys looked like a street gang with their slick ducktail haircuts and sleeveless T-shirts, and they knew the ways of the street. But they had also found things in Scouting that interested them. The activities at Philmont were exciting to them; they wanted to do everything there was to do. The burly old leader talked roughly to the boys and spoke in a hardened growl, but his toughness was largely faked, we all knew. The boys liked him a lot. How great, we thought, that this old grizzly would do something like this just because he wanted to. He's probably the neighborhood cop or a bricklayer or a trucker, we guessed. Someone got around to asking him his line of work—he was an engineer, mechanical and electrical.

Another man we remembered was the "Baltimore Oriole." He had a name, and we knew it at one time, but it was easier to refer to him by his baseball cap which he never left behind. He was about forty and did some desk job in Baltimore, like accounting for a big corporation or something. The other leader, Leo something, was of the same variety. The group was a couple of days out and on their way to the Baldy country. All the Oriole could do was moan and complain. The hikes were too long, trail food wasn't fit to eat, it was a crime to dump people out in a mess like this. We got enough of his griping and were glad to see the group hike out. They could go be miserable someplace else.

A week later the group came back through Ponil to spend their last night on the trail, and the leaders were different men. The Baltimore Oriole was still talking all the time, but now it was about Baldy and what beautiful country this was. He enthused to anybody who would listen about the country they had seen and the times they had had. Later in the summer we got a letter from the Oriole, still in the clouds about his Philmont expedition. Leo showed up at Philmont one day with his family on their vacation trip. He had to show them this country.

There was a good deal of satisfaction along through the summer in making Ponil the kind of camp groups could like and being the kind of staff they would respect. It was hard to make Ponil much of a Scout camp, so we felt pretty cool whenever we were doing it right.

Buzz Clemmons sat parked at an angle on the grass in front of the office in his old, gray panel wagon. He drove a ways up the road and stopped, then wheeled around and drove past the cabin toward the dining hall. He halted there, put the truck in gear, and drove back to the office. Clemmons was triggering for the best spot in Ponil to pick up radio messages from Dan Beard Camp, where a boy had been called in missing. There were four hours of good daylight left, and Buzz was worried.

The Assistant Director had driven out to Ponil in response to a call that a boy named Bruce had been sent to gather breakfast firewood and never came back. It was a while before he was missed and another hour before a runner reached Ponil to phone the message in. Dan Beard was a little outpost in the far northern corner of the ranch. It had no communications of its own, but a commissary truck with a radio unit had come up on a run and was staying to relay messages. Now it was four o'clock and beginning to sink in that the boy was really lost.

Clemmons called around to a few places in headquarters and had a search going by five. A half dozen cowboys from the ranch department drove into Ponil with horse trailers in tow. Near Ponil the smooth government road ended, so the cowboys parked their trucks, mounted their ponies, and rode toward Dan Beard. While they scoured the hills between there and Ponil, the Dan Beard staff went over their camp area. Buzz kept listening to his C.B., but it was silent. The riders searched into twilight, but they found no sign. At dark they rode in to quit for the night.

They loaded their horses by starlight, then drove back out the way they had come, and the boy became more alone than he had ever been.

The Philmont people have never liked losing track of campers, but this time they really cringed. Bruce was a small thirteen-year-old with a spastic condition. Thirteen was too young to be at Philmont in the first place, but to be wandering around in that kind of country alone with a physical handicap could be disastrous. The health lodge medical staff screened all of the campers as they came through headquarters, and ordinarily a Scout with any kind of serious affliction would be held off the trail. They started to hold Bruce off this time too, but his dad was one of the group's leaders and the Philmont trip was something he wanted his boy to have. So he pleaded the boy's case, wanting to be responsible himself for whatever could happen, and Bruce was sent along. Now he was lost.

The boondocks around Dan Beard Camp were not good country to be lost in at night. It was mottled with sinkholes, choppy with the rocky canyon ledges, and widely separated from other settlements. There were long rows of cliffs where a man could walk off into space in the dark. There were old stock ponds and stagnant lakes, and to the north there was the unpatrolled territory of government land stretching north toward Colorado. It would be easy for a spastic boy to tumble down a rocky slope or drown trying to scoop up water from one of the ponds.

The leaders came up to the Long House as usual for an evening of bull and coffee drinking, but all of our minds were on the lost boy. Everything that could happen to him aside from getting found seemed bad; at best he was shivering through a forty-degree night in a T-shirt, he was hungry, and he was scared. Or something worse might have happened to him. When the last of the Scouters had gone, we blew out the lantern and picked our way back across the creek to our cabin noticing that the darkness was very dark tonight and the chill was really cold and a boy out by himself would be very much alone.

The new morning carried over nothing of the unreasoned, shotgun atmosphere of the search the day before. Men at headquarters had been at work and an organized team would go out looking today. Detailed plans were laid and a search force taking in every possible resource was ready to get the boy found. The convoy of searchers that passed through Ponil Canyon was a long and varied one that lasted throughout the day. We had not finished breakfast when the horsemen drove up in front of the dining hall, unloaded, and rode out again. Before long came a school bus load of earth scientists, teachers who learned geology in the field while they showed Scout groups how the land came to look like it did. Most of the men had come dressed for work, clad in field clothes and hats to stop the sun, and toting along such items as canteens, lunches, and field glasses. Pickups ferried them over the rough jeep road from Ponil to Dan Beard.

Still more came to help. There were pickups and panel wagons and jeeps stacked with off-duty Rangers and whatever staff men could be mustered in headquarters. Another pilgrimage wound its way to Dan Beard through North Ponil Canyon. A commissary truck rumbled through carrying food and supplies for the searchers. Even a boat was towed through to drag the shallow lakes around Dan Beard. Dave Shumway took two others from our camp and went up, and other nearby camps made similar treks. Occasional loners and hiking pairs trickled through Ponil all day, some of them sincerely wanting to be of help, others with private hunches where the boy would be, and still more who seemed to be seeking adventure or just curious about about the uproar. Ranching Superintendent Bill Littrell circled overhead in a light plane.

Buzz Clemmons headquartered himself in the ramshackle cabin at Dan Beard, a map of the area in front of him and a radio transceiver nearby. The search planning took a rationale that a spastic boy could in no way have gotten more than three miles from the camp. With this in mind, Clemmons blocked off sections of the map right around Dan Beard, each one to be shaded in when every foot of it had been gone over. Larry Murphy, a young history prof and Philmont summer man of several years, was set over the search party. Across the sectors to be covered he laid out broad swaths that could be handled at one pass by the groups of men. Larry lined them up, and as he gave the commands, they walked abreast across the long rows like a regiment of Chinese seeding the rice fields. Where there were trees and rock forms in the way, the men would take care to keep their lines covered, peering out over every plot of every acre so that it could be known for a fact if a sector had been searched, Bruce was not there. In Dan Beard itself, men looked under shrubs and sacked the buildings and scanned up in the trees to see that the boy was not hiding. By noon most of the territory around the camp had been searched thoroughly enough that anyone within four or five miles of it should at least have been able to hear a voice of a searcher.

With every new failure Bruce's dad felt worse. He damned himself for having brought his boy out here and refused food, saying that Bruce couldn't eat so he wouldn't eat either. He leaned over a cup of coffee and stared into the splintery cabin walls while the radio nearby squawked gibberish. Two chaplains drove up into camp in a jeep to offer the father what they could, but there was not much to say, and one of them strode out to walk in the line of searchers. Medics came too, and they did get the man to take something to relax him. When the day wore long, the father was driven down to headquarters where he could rest, but with the promise that he could live by the control center radio.

Ponil was never quiet, but today it was busier than ever with the continuous flow of rescue traffic. Once in a while headquarters would call with a message we should give to some particular man if we could waylay him on the road. The rest of Bruce's group hiked through Ponil on their way to Pueblano Camp during the morning, having resumed their trip after the day's delay. They only stopped for supplies and water, then hiked out again, a few of them asking whether anything had been seen of Bruce.

The sun receded over the upper reaches of the canyon and the day went on for a couple of twilight hours. It wasn't until the last hour before absolute darkness that the forms of jeeps and men began moving down from the Dan Beard cutoff into Ponil. The earth scientists came in with their hats bent around in casual formations evolved through hours of hiking and their dirty shirts half-buttoned and blowing loose around their hairy middle-aged bellies. Many of them carried rock samples they had picked up during the day. They were tired and down. They climbed aboard the school bus that was waiting for them and left for headquarters. Many more searchers poured down out of the hills, with some of the mountain vehicles ferrying the stretch two and three times to bring down all of the hundred or so who had accumulated. We watched the procession and wondered again how it was that one spastic boy could elude all these regiments of outdoorsmen.

The third wave of searchers started soon after dawn when a helicopter sputtered its way up the canyon toward Dan Beard. It settled into a channel between the canyon sides and blustery gusts swept up as it moved low over the ground. It veered toward Dan Beard, then made a few slow passes over the country below camp before chopping away over the ridges and out of sight. The earth scientists were back, and so were many of the others who had been this way before. They no longer looked beyond and anticipated, but were set for the tedium of a routine. The men were tired from yesterday's all-day walk and were not especially looking forward to another. They crowded onto the pickups and jeeps and bounded up the rutty road to Dan Beard.

The helicopter skipped across Bonito Canyon and angled northward over the leveled badlands above the camp. Peering out the bubble dome from a compartment just behind the cockpit was Ray H. Bryan. Bryan carried the title of General Manager of the Phillips Properties, a position which put him squarely in charge of Philmont and all its operations—camping, ranching, and training— as well as the running of the Philtower Office Building which Philmont held in Tulsa as a supplementary source of income. Bryan had followed Philmont's development from the beginning—he had been a friend of Waite Phillips, fished with him in the Rayado. He was one of Scouting's men who came when Phillips wanted to make a gift of his land. Then as an engineer for the national organization, Bryan had designed the first log buildings for Philturn Rockymountain Scout Camp. Ray Bryan was the top executive, and he had financial and managerial duties that kept him in another part of the country as often as at the ranch.

But today the graying executive would welcome no visitors to his office. He would sign no big checks and would direct no memoranda to his management team. He scanned the ground as the helicopter crossed over the search area and strayed off north moving away from Philmont. It eased on, five miles, six, seven miles from Dan Beard. Ray Bryan's stare found a T-shirted boy waving from below. Bryan shouted into his headset to turn back and set down. The pilot made no move and the machine went ahead. Bryan raved on into a dead microphone and the chopper continued north. Bryan beat on the window between the two sections and caught the pilot's attention. The helicopter swooped around and hovered down to pick the boy up. The men pulled him in, then the chopper whisked away toward headquarters while Bryan radioed that Bruce was found.

The helicopter put down near the health lodge in headquarters where his dad gave thanks. The medics were surprised at the boy's condition. After two nights of wandering and a hike no one thought he could make, Bruce was fine—just very hungry and a little weak. Bruce, it happened, had remembered his scouting and had used it. He had found shelter both nights under rock overhangs along the bluffs. Knowing that the water could be impure, he shunned the ponds and drank only what water he could catch when it rained.

At headquarters they didn't drop the matter just yet. If there was something to be learned from it, the Director wanted to learn it. Larry Murphy was assigned to chronicle the details of the three days and describe the search techniques and how they might be improved. He would set down the roles of search participants, tell of the problems they faced, and outline the needs of a general search plan. The men would take this experience and iron out a plan for reacting to missing person alarms and for carrying off search-and-rescue operations. Bruce stayed in the health lodge for a few days, then he and his dad headed for home, the promise of an unforgettable adventure fulfilled. Philmont would not forget either.

One thing we never were at Ponil was bored. When we worked we worked and when we played we played, but we never were inclined to just sit around and let the time pass. We were a pretty active bunch, and we found things to do in our spare time.

Early in the summer we spent a lot of hours working up songs. After supper each evening we would drag out our instruments and set up singing for awhile. Everybody had a few favorites; we tried them all and made some of them sound pretty good. When we got to where we could execute a bunch of them reasonably well, we started making the rounds of the campsites every evening. After supper we would take our guitars and stroll up through the long canyon and into the various troop sites. We would just sort of visit around and make friends among the groups and sing a couple of songs while they worked at cooking supper or cleaning up. Whenever the campers liked our singing, or in some cases when we offered to leave, the boys would throw money. We began encouraging that practice, and at the summer's end we divided about a dollar and twenty in pennies and nickels.

Another thing we did was rock climbing and rappelling. Mountaineering is a kind of sport that few people know about, but it is easy to get hooked on. Bob Mathias and Mark Oyster ran Ponil's mountaineering program—a new activity at Philmont—and now and then they would take some of us up the canyon to try some more difficult crags. We learned to pick our way up vertical surfaces on the outcrops by going up cracks and chimneys. Chimneys are upright crevices wide enough for a man to get into with some freedom of movement, but not so wide that he can't somehow touch both sides. Attached to a safety line and belayed by a friend above, we could wedge our bodies across the chimney, sometimes stretching spread-eagle across a precipice to work our way up. There is something exciting about the tension of holding each muscle taut against the rocks to maintain some kind of equilibrium and about depending on each foot placement and on the slightest ripples and irregularities in the rock to pass, at every step, a new test of whether you will hold or fall.

Rappelling is something that shows up in military sabotage movies and spy shows once in a while; it looks easy the way the heroes come bounding down the side of a sheer cliff or a high wall, sliding free down the loose hanging rope and bouncing off the wall every fifteen feet. But rappelling, although a thrill, is tricky to learn. It takes some nerve to back off over a cliff and lean parallel to the ground while balancing your whole weight on one rope. We rappelled off a couple of good-sized outcrops, one that went straight down, and the other an overhang where you faced the extra hazzard of getting over a jutting ledge at the top, then sliding through space along the rope while controlling your fall with a one-hand grip on the rope. Bob and Mark about had to push some of us off the top at first, but after we had gotten the feel of it, we would stay on the rocks until full darkness made us quit.

Sometimes we could get into some fairly good capers down at the horse barns. Most of the time we would just practice roping on the fence posts or pitch horseshoes, but when we were feeling a little bit wild we would run a few burros into the corral and do some rodeoing. Once you had caught a burro you could put a halter on him, bringing the lead rope around his neck and tying the loose end up by the other jaw to form a rein. This does not mean that the burro would know what you wanted him to do by your motions with the reins, or that he would care to cooperate if he did know; the rope just gave you something to hang onto.

Getting on a burro bareback is not too easy since there are no stirrups or anything. If the burro is very big, you have to throw yourself up across his back on your belly and then wriggle around until you can get your other leg over his back. Once you are on, the burro will do one of two things. Either he will run completely wild, or he will just stand there and ignore any command to go. I always favored the first response, because if the burro didn't go on his own, the watchers would take it upon themselves to see that he did go, and spooking him from behind or swatting a tender area of his body would usually be enough to send him into orbit.

On my first ride the burro was in a mood to run and he went into a fit, galloping around the corral and looking for a way to get me off him. He ran me under the eaves of the barn and through a small herd of burros bunched up in one corner of the corral. Then he charged for the fence and that was enough for me. As he plummeted into it, I grabbed onto the fence rail and got away pretty well unscathed.

We went two or three times around trying to make decent mounts of the ornery, mean-headed packjacks. Kermit the cook did pretty well. Although Kermit spoke in a refined tongue uncommon to the rest of the camp staff and spent most of his spare time sitting on the porch perusing volumes of Dostoevski and other literary giants, he had a wiry toughness that kept him battering around upon his burro's spine when most of us would have been done in.

The next time I got on one, it was a bummer. After a short run the burro started quick-stopping and went into a kind of spastic bucking routine. His pitching wasn't violent or anything, but I could feel myself slowly going down the tube. Every time he did throw his head down and kick back, I would slide a little more forward on his back and on up over his shoulders. Finally I was out on his neck, which was narrow and bony and didn't work at all as a place to sit, so I tumbled and hit the ground on my tail bone. The burro dashed his hoofs in front of my face a few times, then galloped on off. Actually, if you could keep from getting kicked in the head when the burro threw you, it was considered a good ride.

Four or five times a summer the mountain men will come down out of their camps for a vacation of a day or two. There is plenty to do. If Philmont is in your blood, you could hike the whole summer and not see enough of it. Beyond that, New Mexico has some roads that will lead you away, and most of us were bent on seeing what we could find along those roads.

All within a half day's travel of the ranch are the La Mesa Park Racetrack at Raton, Bandelier National Monument, Santa Fe, Taos, and Colorado Springs. There are Carlsbad and the caverns, Wheeler Peak, and Pikes Peak, and a dozen other things a young man might want to see. At the mountain resort of Red River, there are even some girls—if you happen to be in junior high. That there are such attractions nearby is partly incidental, for even if they were not there we would still probably have been drawn to the open road. And so on any day in the summer you will find some of us standing along U.S. 64, hair blowing down the canyon and thumbs pointing up the highway toward whatever is there.

I was dead set on seeing more of the country this summer. During two others, I had hardly strayed from Philmont, and never very far. I wanted very much to see Santa Fe, the centuries old city whose development had been shaped by so long a continuum of cultural influences that included Spanish, Indians, Mexicans, Texans, and the eastern born American pioneers; a city forged of adobe walls and mission bells and Indian copper.

Lee Heine, who was from Wisconsin, was Ponil's quartermaster. With his short build, dark hair, bushy eyebrows, and horn-rimmed glasses set low over darker eyes, he looked the part of a mobster more than a Scout leader; but Lee was a good one and a good friend. Early in the summer we began talking about a jaunt down to Santa Fe, and we set up a long day off at the same time. We planned some of the details and quizzed guys who had been there about places to stay overnight and things to see and do. Lee got us a trail tent and we packed our bedrolls along.

The night before leaving we rode into headquarters to get our money and equipment all set. Very early in the morning we packed up and got a short hop into Cimarron and walked along the highway hoping for a ride. Within the first minutes a rickety, red pickup pulled over. We threw our packs in and climbed in the back with a half dozen little Chicano farm kids. One of them offered us a cinder block to sit on and we spent the next hour viewing the world from just that perspective. We bounced on the truck bed and watched the road we had covered disappear. Cimarron Canyon was obscured by a thick white fog that isolated the truck in its own little bubble of visibility. The intrigue of the ride wore off as a cold wind whipped in and out of the truck bed, and we began to hope the driver would turn off so that we could try again. At the meadow resort of Eagle Nest he pulled off and pointed toward Red River. We thanked him and tossed our bags off, then jumped down behind them.

We walked up the highway again, turning to show our thumbs whenever we heard a car and hoping this time for a heated sedan. We walked through Eagle Nest and started across the rolling meadow that separated the Cimarron Mountains from the Carson National Forest. A Volkswagen went by us, then the brake lights went on and it pulled off onto the shoulder. We jogged up to it and a soldier got out and opened the trunk for us to stow the bags. He was heading home on leave from Fort Sill and had stopped at the sight of our Scout clothes. He was a leader on post and told us about his troop, and we talked Scouting to Espanola. As we rode, the mountains swirled to a summit at Palo Flechado Pass, then dropped into the old village of Taos. We crossed the Rio Grande and followed it across the kind of rolling sand and cactus country we had envisioned as New Mexico. At Espanola the soldier went out of his way to drive us out the Santa Fe highway to where we could catch another ride in the right direction.

The summer traffic was running heavy on Route 64, and we had not much more than slung our packs over our shoulders and watched the Volks sputter back through town when a Volkswagen van stopped for us. Lee opened the door and a graying, professional-looking man spoke to us. He turned and reached back over the seat to move over several paintings that cluttered the back of the van. We were glad to hear him say he would be going to downtown Santa Fe; we would be there by noon. The man was an artist. His long, swept-back hair, baggy pants, and sport shirt with long sleeves rolled to the elbow made him look the part. The man was full of talk and excited about life in general, yet he was not a neon-eyed surrealist. He was down to earth. His eyes scanned the landscape and appreciated it as something more than an interval between towns. He enjoyed telling us about Santa Fe, about the places we should go and features we shouldn't miss. He named off a dozen art galleries and museums and we tried to remember them all; he described them with such fluent verve and personal knowledge that we were intrigued to see them too.

Hitchhiking was one of the great things about the Philmont life, and it furnished dozens of experiences that I would not have missed. Hitchhiking has never been a very glorious way to travel and became less so with the spread of the mass automobile. It has about lost any aura of respectability it may once have had when none but the well-to-do had cars. Like most of the others at Philmont, I would never have thought of hitchhiking at home and probably would not now. But at Philmont there was no other way to get around and no one to remind you of the dozens of highwayers who get robbed and their heads bashed every year.

Hitchhiking right around the ranch was not what it would have been anywhere else. The people who lived right around Cimarron either worked at Philmont or at least knew it was there. To many of them a Scout uniform was a good enough reason to pick a kid up, and I doubt whether any of them ever regretted it. Once you had thumbed the short rides around Cimarron, it was only natural to thumb a little farther and a little farther still until you were at ease traveling all around northeastern New Mexico with anyone who would stop.

But the really great thing about hitchhiking was the people. People who pick up riders cannot begin to be lumped together. I rode in limousines, cattle transports, dump trucks, cement mixers, and sports cars. The drivers included laborers, truck drivers, blacks, whites, Indians, cowboys, doctors, and tourists, and the one thing they had in common was a genuine liking for people. Introverts don't often stop. For a city boy used to the orderly life of classes and bus schedules and school bells and clocks, the highway life is a glimpse of living. Stick your thumb out and something will happen. You don't plan out a trip and take it. You stick your thumb out and let it take you where it will. I was a long way from Philmont when I first forked over my savings for a car, but I could not at the time help but think of the loss of an excuse to hitchhike. I regretted that loss then and I regret it now, because although I could, in theory, leave the car parked any day and take to the highway, the feeling would not be the same. It would lack authenticity.

We cruised past the opera house on the eastern limits of Santa Fe, then drove down into the crowded downtown and parked in front of a tan Spanish-style art gallery. The artist told us where to look him up in Taos and wished us a good trip. We shouldered our packs and took off down one of the narrow streets.

The town centered on a little plaza with walks and statuary. Adobe walls and jutting beams ran down every row of shops. The town wallowed in leisure, its laziness hidden under the shady trees around the plaza. The sidewalks were but narrow ledges against the buildings and parking meters were set neatly in the middle of them, so that we kept one eye to the front as we walked. We wandered around until we discovered the bus station, where we changed into some other clothes and packed our stuff into one of the baggage lockers. After eating we stopped for a handful of maps and leaflets at a tourism booth on the plaza, then set off to look at Santa Fe.

We studied the map and oriented ourselves for the Palace of the Governors, which lay to the east of the square and looked out onto the plaza. I don't know how many governors ever lived there, but when they say "palace," they are using the word liberally. If I had ever put the governor up in something like that, I don't believe I would be advertising it. The building was a long, one-story flat with the characteristic adobe walls of Spanish southwestern style and a plain cement floor. The inside walls were cracked and paint was peeling off the ceiling. It was fixed up as a museum, the present governor having declined to live in so hallowed a place, we supposed. The display cases were filled with everything from Indian wares to World War II artifacts. Out front on the long porch various Indians sat against the wall, their dull woolen blankets pulled close around against August's breezes and their merchandise of trinkets spread on the walk before the milling vacationers.

The main art museum was just up the street a block off the plaza so we browsed through it before heading away from the downtown area. We turned west in search of the state capitol, the location of which we weren't too sure. We looked over the map and wandered off in what seemed to be the general direction of the capitol. We meandered down the back streets and through the barrios, and came upon a dull yellow structure that was the old capitol. It was a squared-off old stucco thing that looked more like an office building than a state house. We wandered through the halls looking for some evidence of grandeur. Instead we found only dim corridors and a janitor who pointed out the new capitol that had been built across the street. On a knoll to the south was a fine, commanding thing that was much more in line with what we thought a state capitol ought to look like. The broad green lawn led up to a high building that was round and sat above and away over the surrounding territory. Set around in the space of the ground floor were displays of flags and all kinds of stately ornamentation—great seals and such. There were legislative chambers richly paneled in dark woods and lined plushly. Upstairs the governor was entertaining guests in his glass-front suite.

We walked down one of the narrow streets to a string of the real hardcore tourist joints. The first ones we came to were the "Oldest House in the United States" and the "Oldest Church" in the country. I don't know how many "oldest" houses and churches there are in this country, but I'm pretty sure these weren't the only ones. The "oldest house" was but a tiny adobe cell off a souvenir shop. Once you got in, you found out that only the floor was really part of the original house, and the much-celebrated floor bore a remarkable likeness to any other barren plot of ground. The rest of the hut was dingy, its walls left scarred and crumbling, we guessed, to add to the effect of its alleged age. The "oldest church" was a small Catholic chapel down the street. The pictures in the little gallery inside showed that it had burned and been torn down and rebuilt so many times that it no longer resembled the original building. The newer facade though, with its intricate cornice and ancient mission effect, made the church look delightfully quaint for the tourists. At one side a souvenir shop had been built on, and you could buy all kinds of "oldest church" curios and religious souvenirs. There were rows and cases of crucifixes, postcards, shrines, and pictures, each decorated with the inscription, "Oldest Church in the United States, Santa Fe, New Mexico."

Further down the street toward the plaza was the Spiral Staircase in another church. It was acclaimed the "Eighth Wonder of the World," and there are a lot of those around too. To get to the miraculous steps we followed a narrow garden path around behind the church and through a small courtyard to the rear entrance where there was a nun on duty. The sister had a tape recorder loaded with a little historical narrative all about the church and the staircase. She was mostly snubbed by the boorish tourists who brushed on by to get in, so Lee and I constructed a pleasant face and stood at the door listening to how the church was started by Father Moreno in the seventeenth century, then the balcony was added in 1798, et cetera, et cetera. We dropped some change in her coin box and finally got into the sanctuary.

At the back of the church was a balcony, and winding up to it was a staircase without any visible center pole or supporting beams. The tourists were more or less crowded around, staring at it as though it was supposed to suddenly come to life and dance or perform some feat to entertain them. But of course it just stood there in its centuries old suspension. The stairs were permanently roped off, which led us to think that they weren't doing a whole lot of good as a link between the ground floor and the balcony. Or maybe the people didn't quite trust the structural soundness of the eighth wonder. It was a real nice staircase all right, but Lee and I couldn't exactly see where it deserved a place in the tourist's guide to the sights of Santa Fe.

Maybe it was the tourists, like us, who made the places seem extraneous. After all, who could appreciate anything when viewing it from amid a circus crowd of sunshades and ball caps and camera cases and cranky children. At any rate, we could not quite seem to get into the spirit of things.

The afternoon was getting along and we strolled toward the plaza wondering where we would spend the night. We sat down on a curb to consider the possibilities. There were no hotels around that suited our standards at a price we wanted to pay; we didn't want to spend money on a room anyway. We asked around about any state or national parks that might be close by, but there weren't any. We mulled over all of the ideas we could come up with, but none of them seemed practical. We got tired of thinking about it and went in and looked at a movie just to get off the streets for a while. Then we would eat and get our stuff from the bus station, and head for the outskirts of town to find a place to camp.

We walked back through town at dusk, still wondering where we were going. We took a street that, according to the map, would lead us to the edge of town in about a mile. While we walked it the sun sank behind us. We turned up a country road and walked a ways, and the daylight dulled to a twilight that only illuminated the contrasts between the dark juniper shrubs and the lighter sky and sandy-colored hills. Lee pointed out a rough dirt road coursing its way up a roadside hill. We followed it off the unfenced highway and up to a little plateau where we found the place.

The hill overlooked the whole city of Santa Fe, its lights spread far around us in a broad, glittering fan. We looked for landmarks we could recognize and saw that we had come out around the back side of the hill and looped back toward town, so that we ended up only a few blocks from downtown. At the head point of the ridge were a tall wooden cross and an altar that made the place seem the setting of an Easter pageant or something. We got off a little from the road and searched out a smooth place to pitch camp. We found a good low spot where we would not be seen by any police car or anyone who might happen to come up the road, and there we set up our trail tent. The moon was up and reflecting softly off the light-shaded rocky hillsides. Before turning in we sat for a long time at the edge of the hill looking down across the galaxy of city lights. There were clear starry skies all around, earth below, and summer breezes that warmed the night and made it friendly. The surroundings made for an occasion so enjoyable that I knew at the time I was enjoying it.

We slept until the sun was well up and heating the canvas tent sides. We rolled up the camp and packed it away, then walked to the knoll to take a last look at the sweep of Santa Fe. We walked down past the cross and bushwhacked down the hill toward town, cutting through a couple of big yards where a trespass might not be noticed. Along the streets on the plaza the shopkeepers were out sweeping off their walks and opening for the day.

We made our way back to the bus station and walked from the sunny morning street into a dank air of cigarette smoke and industrial cleanser and human sweat and bus fumes. The scene was always the same. The faces were always the same—ageless, tired, fixed in a stupor brought on by too many hours of riding and waiting and riding and waiting. We crammed our bags into a locker again, dropped a quarter in the slot, pulled the key, and went off to finish our visit.

Eating in restaurants was one of the luxuries of a trip

like ours. This morning's breakfast was especially good, not only for the chilled melon and hot scrambled eggs, but because the service was so slow. The virtue in this was in the padded booths and air-conditioned freshness that made such a gratifying contrast to rocky ground and streets. We dawdled over our coffee before heading out to look in some craft shops.

When everything worth seeing was seen, we made one more stop at the bus station. We changed back into our Scouting clothes and packed away the rest, then combed our hair until we were the kind of clean-cut hitchhikers that ought to get picked up. We shouldered our packs and walked out the highway a piece. It was nearly an hour before we got the first ride, a six-mile haul in a paving truck. That was typical of the rest of the day, most of which was spent walking the pavement and watching the cars whiz by us and out of sight toward where we wanted to be. But we didn't worry about being late. We were highwayers, and whenever we got home, we would be on time.

5

Of all the mountain camps, Harlan is a special one to me. I loved that place, both for its beauty and for its aloneness. Harlan was set high up the side of Deer Lake Mesa, tucked into one of the meadow terraces along the north face of the mesa. Against the slope were a rectangular board cabin and a low cook shack behind it. A flag flew from its lone pinnacle in the meadow, and at the far side of the terrace ran a low ridge rimming the camp area. Harlan, with its back to the mesa, looked out over all of the country to the other three sides. From our place we could look down the meadow and straight out into space toward a horizon of far distant peaks.

The little ridge across the meadow gave a wide panorama of the north country. Whenever there was something I wanted to think over or I just wanted the feeling that I got from looking out over the mountain country, I would amble over and walk along the length of the rim ridge and look far up into the north, out across Cimarron Canyon and over the tiers of ridges and canyons that went to the far skyline. On the other side was Harlan, laid out in its brief mountain clearing—the tent-dotted campsites with smoke rising from them and the sounds of campers, the burro pens, the cabin and paths where we hurried so much of the time. The low-crested ridge sat above it all and was an unfailing quencher for frustration or boredom. There was one more place, an eastern bluff at the very end of the string of campsites, where we could look to the east across the plains beyond Philmont and down upon the village of Cimarron. We were situated in a high perch where we saw and felt and breathed the mountains. At Harlan, you knew you were in the backcountry.

Harlan's staff population fluctuated a lot during the summer, but there were mainly three of us who ran the camping end of the operation. I was Camp Director. John Winniford was the conservationist and took care of things that needed fixing around camp. One of his jobs was to make a half-mile pilgrimage down the road and across the bull pasture every few days to start the water pump that sat in a low, out of the way hollow. The old clunker that we had was contrary about starting up, but John tinkered around and soon knew all of its eccentricities. He would humor the stubborn engine until it kicked off into its cycle, then head back up the slope and leave it to run until the calculated amount of gas gave out.

Dave McNeel ran a map and compass program for the benefit of the first-day groups who were about to strike out across the countryside on their own. Between his programs Dave was forever over in the campsites talking to the groups and helping them out, and generally making friends as fast as they came in. Then we had a cowboy by the name of Sam Bennett, who looked after the herd of burros pastured down below the little ridge at the lower end of camp. All through the summer Sam kept us entertained, and sometimes riled, at his cowboy ways of doing things. Besides the regular bunch, we had earth science men coming up one or two at a time for week-long field trips of exploring and taking the campers on geology hikes.

We were hardly aware of the Scout Ranch. Harlan was an easily forgotten camp, and we liked being forgotten. It was out of the way and not very accessible. It was hardly worth the trouble to take a vehicle with four-wheel drive and come around by the highway, then maneuver up the mountain trail to visit one small camp, when most of the other camps were along more logical and better-traveled routes, so the sanitation officer, the sector director, and the other extensions of administrative structure seldom reached us. We had no radio or telephone in camp either, so we escaped a lot of the trivial concerns we would otherwise have been vulnerable to. We drank coffee with the leaders each night by the yellow light of kerosene lanterns, and were glad that we had no generator that would be breaking down. We had no neighbor camps to speak of and had little contact with anybody except the daily camping groups and the occasional staff men who drifted through, so we were glad to see the people who did come our way and we found friends among them almost every day.

At Harlan we could feel the mountain country and we became part of it. Within the first couple of weeks we had taken on new senses. The tents and open-air cook shack that we lived out of left us pretty much out in the summer's weather, and we began to know its every shade and change. The raw mountain weather had many moods that became part of how we felt. We breathed in the dry air of clean, sunny mornings, and the fresh-chilled pine scent after hailstorms had bruised the trees, and all of the breezes that drifted our way between them. We were well acquainted with daylight and darkness and the nuances that came between one and the other, and we lived by them. After-supper excursions and late chores were paced to be finished by nightfall. We knew some of the deer who came down regularly to graze in our meadow and to browse on the shrubs up by our tents, and the few bears who made night visits from time to time; sometimes they acted as if they knew us. No one had tamed this country, or imposed insulating barricades to protect the civilized places from the unbroken wilds. We were just part of the life that grew on Deer Lake Mesa.

Harlan was my camp. As Camp Director, I was responsible for the staff, the water supply, the bears, the programs, the campsites, the sanitation system, and everything else that walked, talked, or just sat there in Harlan Camp. My days were filled with dealing with group leaders, supervising the staff, testing water, ordering supplies, doctoring sunburn blisters, washing my share of the dishes, sending in various reports, and just walking around camp picking up trash and fixing things that didn't look exactly right.

My job carried some responsibilities that I had never

noticed a Camp Director having until I was one. Although I was in charge of Harlan, I was also accountable for a lot of things. I had to be sober about looking out for the campers' safety and about dealing with each leader's problems and about watching how other people did their jobs—things that had never caused me much concern before. The kinds of problems and decisions that we had so casually passed on to the one in charge in years before now came straight to me. I would often find myself mulling over some situation that was not just like I would want it to be, weighing whether it would be wiser just now to lay back or to jump in.

But I also had an opportunity that not so many people of my age had, the opportunity to run a total operation and be responsible for its success or failure, to lay plans, to prepare, to set a direction, to lead. I had a chance to make the kind of camp that would be something memorable to the Scouts who came and help younger staff men grow and develop in their sense of responsibility and their affinity for working with people—and grow some myself. I had watched other Camp Directors work, watched their abilities and their mistakes, and I had given pretty much thought to the kind of place Harlan ought to be, but I soon learned that the opportunity I had was one that is always bigger than the man. The creativity that could be put into making Harlan better was infinite, and my ability usually seemed very finite. Nevertheless, I had the chance to take the resources that were there and see what I could make of them. I had a chance to take charge of Harlan Camp and make it as good as we were able.

Bears are sort of a small anxiety in the back of everyone's mind. They seldom do harm and generally they stay clear of people. The dangerous thing about bears is that they are always hungry, and the Scouts always have food. Philmont bears have seen a lot of people, and they sense their own physical superiority. They will wander into camps and get into any food left lying open; some will even prowl into tents if the smell of food is strong. Most of the bears, though, are docile and can be controlled to some degree. Rangers train their groups to tie their food high between two trees to keep it from harm during the night and tell the boys to keep candy and food away from their tents. And if a bear does come around, noise will scare him away. The meeting of bears and Scouts has made for plenty of incidents and stories that the boys will remember for a long time. Publicly, bears are comical creatures that lumber around and dabble in mischief. But privately, most of us have had our doubts, and one of the first questions a newly arrived Scout leader might ask when there is no one around to laugh is: "Say, what are those bears *really* like?"

On our third day at Harlan there was a lot to be done. We had trails to check, campsites to rework, programs to develop, and a dozen other things to do before the camping season began. John Winniford and Dave McNeel went out to cover a couple of trails while I waited in camp for our first supply delivery. John and Dave came in a little before noon, and the rattly green ton and a half commissary truck came rumbling up the road, gnashing its lower gears against the crude mountain road. The three of us fell out to meet the truck and unload its cargo. We took off the wire crates that held our food for the next few days and, one by one, carried them around to the rustic kitchen cabin behind the longer commissary building. The little kitchen was a wooden cubicle with a sort of adirondack roof that slanted off farther in back than in front. It was just a summer hut, having only three board walls and a big screen window plus two screen doors to keep the flies out. After setting all of the food inside we four stood around the truck to shoot the bull for awhile. John, Dave, and I had seen almost nobody from the outside world since being left up in the hills, and we welcomed the opportunity to talk to anyone who might chance to come up the winding mountain road.

A bear appeared across the meadow and came ambling toward the cabins. John and Dave hadn't seen loose bears and were kind of wondering if there were any around and what they were like. I kind of was too, because although I had seen quite a few of the docile type that sniffed around and posed for pictures, they had not ever won me for a friend. The new animal did nothing to change my mind. He was big and shrouded in thick fur, and walked in a slow, deliberate path. He, or she, just checked everything out in his good time, going wherever he pleased. He zigzagged his way across the meadow in a lackadaisical way, but his general direction was toward us and the cabins.

Even in the excitement we did do enough thinking to see what was about to happen, or at least one thing that was about to happen. I dashed into the kitchen and latched both doors, which, in view of the bear's great strength and lack of regard for such folly as screen doors, soon seemed a foolish thing to have done. The bear had the scent of our food, and he began to focus that aroma right in on the buildings. He ambled on toward us at his leisure, pausing now and then to take a closer sniff at something along the way. We had seen enough. We began to holler and beat on pans and make as much racket as we could raise. Bears, being creatures of the wild, were supposed to be frightened off by such things. Ours had not gotten the word on that. The most attention he would pay us was a side glance.

We needn't have worried, for the commissary truck driver, as luck would have it, was an expert on a number of things, just one of which happened to be bear control. He took an ax out of the truck and thought that he would take the bear on hand-to-hand. I pointed out a few of the drawbacks in his plan, and after a time, he put the ax back in the truck. By now the bear was at the cabin and really casing it out. He stood up on his hind paws and his head towered above the roof line. We piled on the truck and drove toward the cabin, revving the engine and blasting the horn. The bear remained cool; he was going about his business just as though we had gone to the beach for the weekend. While we kept on making futile runs at him, the mundane old bear thrust his paw through the screen door and ripped out a nice hole.

Then we gaped while the bear put his woolly hulk through the screen to where our food lay open. He made a couple of selections from one of the baskets and carried them in his teeth, back out the door, off the porch, and up the hill to a spot behind the latrine. In the darkened shade of a thick grove, he worked open the packages and ate. As soon as we dared, we hurried in to put away the rest of the food. When the bear finished his first course, he plodded back down for more. We soon had everything out of reach, but the bear lurked around for another hour before leaving.

I wanted to get to a phone and report the incident. I rode down to the highway with the commissary driver, who had still more advice about how we could keep our bear in hand. Just before I got out at the highway, he suggested that we ought to throw a lighted package of firecrackers at the bear the next time he came around. He would bring us some, in fact. That was the last we ever saw of that particular driver, as I soon wrote the commissary manager letting him know that I would rather not have the driver in Harlan any more. His adventures were not over though. The axman–bear hunter–truck driver turned his truck over the following week and spent the rest of the summer, we were told, stacking cans in the headquarters warehouse.

I got to town and phoned around to different ranch people hoping to get a bear trap lined up. I finally got hold of one office that would at least talk to me. That was the last we would ever hear of it; we thought the ranch men would take us to be city gunsels worked up over nothing and would not do anything. But I was disturbed about this particular bear. He was different from any I had ever met. For one thing he had come during the day, while most bears circulated at night. He was bold and too unafraid of people. Finally, he was huge—bigger than any I had seen. Harlan would be a Scout camp in less than a week, and the idea of so dangerous an animal running loose among the campers and us didn't exactly sit right. I deliberated the matter over a butterscotch malt, then thumbed a ride back out the highway to the Harlan cutoff.

When I got back to Harlan, John had the broken door off its hinges and was repairing the torn screen. Dave had collected the food wrappers strung up along the hillside. By his calculation, the bear had eaten a half dozen Salisbury steaks, two pounds of bacon, two pounds of salami, and two trail breakfasts. We talked about the bear for the rest of the day but really weren't too worried over the one incident. If all the bear wanted was food, we could just keep everything put up and he would quit coming around.

But during the night, we slept through another raid. The bear came back and broke in both screen doors in exactly the same pattern as he had torn the one before. All he had found in the kitchen were a couple of trail lunches, so he had gone out and dumped over the garbage cans and scattered garbage halfway up the hill behind the cabins. One of the cans was still full—and fifty yards into the woods from where it had stood.

The bear thing began to eat on us. This bear had gotten a good meal only the previous morning. He shouldn't have been back for a couple of days. Now there was no way to know when he would come around. It might be night or day, but whenever he did come, the camp would be his. All we could do was secure the food and make noise, and that was not much of a defense. More than anything, none of us wanted to be surprised. We began to walk a big circle around corners that blocked the view. We visited the latrine only in daylight hours or in groups of three, since that was the bear's eating site. The bear was named "Big Bertha," although we went ahead referring to it as "he."

Late in the afternoon Bob Knox and Larry Mesaric of the cattle department drove up the road pulling a trailer behind their pickup, a cagelike trailer that we knew right away was our bear trap. We ran out to make the cowboys welcome. The trap was a cage about seven feet by four, maybe four feet high. It was mounted on an axle with wheels so that it could be towed easily. The cage itself was of heavy chain link webbing stretched over a steel frame. Bob backed the thing up near the kitchen. We dug a couple of holes for the tires to slip down into so that the cage's floor would be at ground level and the bear would have an easier time getting himself caught. Bob crawled inside the trap to bait it. Bob was a classic cowboy, lean and rangy with a low drawl and wide bloodshot eyes that rolled from side to side. He took a handful of lunch meat and stuffed it into the burlap bait bag. Then he scattered some bread slices and fruit around the sack and covered the whole thing with honey. Bob got out and raised up the door to set the trap. A pin held the heavy steel door up until it was released by a tug on the bait sack at the other end of the wire. We tried it out a few times to be sure the tension was just right. We offered the cowboys a cup of coffee and some cookies for their trouble, then sent them down the hill with our genuine thanks.

Although Harlan was geographically the closest camp to town and was within ten miles of headquarters, it was made distant from them by the miles of steep, broken terrain that surrounded the camp. The road that brought the few vehicles into Harlan was out of the way, and unlike most other service roads it did not bring traffic through on the way to other camps. Except in emergencies, Harlan was the only stop on the old backroad. The chaplains, the medics, the Philmont directors frequently visited the more reachable camps, but hardly ever made the inconvenient drive around and up to Harlan. There were no telephone lines into Harlan and we had no electricity, so there was no C.B. radio either.

We would be joined by a wrangler, earth scientists, and a steady flow of campers for most of the summer; but for the time being, we were three alone in a little wilderness settlement of two small cabins and three tents, and we felt a new sense of solitary self-reliance. The lurking presence of the bear made that feeling grow and made us think a little about the prospect of surviving. We no longer took our routine well-being entirely for granted, but gave it some thought, especially at night. The bear's manner had given him a personality, a character. He was intelligent beyond the bounds of primitive instinct, and he had become sinister to us. We sat around a board table in the dull yellowed light of a kerosene lantern and talked of what could happen—What if he gets caught and breaks out of the trap? What if the door falls on his head or legs while he is only partly inside and sends him into a rage? Last summer hadn't a bear been wounded by state hunters and come back the next night to burn down Lover's Leap Camp?

We moved our cots from the wall tents behind the kitchen down to the commissary building for the night. John had been filing down his machete during the day and had it right by his bed ready for combat. The building was dark, and we lay there for a long time listening for the plodding walk and heavy breath of the bear and imagining his head silhouetted in one of the building's windows. We tensed at the sound of every rustling pine and at the mice scampering underneath us. In the morning we found but an empty trap, the bait arranged just as we had left it. There were no tracks around the cabin, no overturned garbage cans. Maybe the bear had gone over the hill for good.

About the middle of the morning "Boss" Sanchez and a couple of his horse wranglers came up to tend the thirty burros pastured at Harlan, since Harlan's permanent wrangler had not shown up yet. A little before lunchtime Bob Knox and Larry Mesaric and Bob's son and daughter rode in from punching cattle in the area. We invited them all for lunch and threw open all the bread and sandwich makings we had. After they had eaten, the cowboys settled down on the back porch and under the shade of some pine trees to let things ride awhile before going back to work. The sun was out and the dust was up, and it was a better afternoon to rest than to work.

Larry was a young country-type cowboy. He got up off the porch, dusted off his jeans, and walked a bowlegged walk up toward the latrine. There was a yell, then Larry came running back down the trail with our bear plodding behind him. Bob spoke low to everybody to sit still on the porch and maybe the bear would go to the trap. The bear headed right for it, and we stayed and watched him walk around out there thirty feet from us. The bear stalked around the outside to the back of the trap where the food was. He put his paws up on the trap and stood up shaking the wire mesh. Then he padded around the whole trap casing it out. He was cautious and would not go in with the audience staring on.

The animal tired of playing with the trap and turned toward the kitchen. The crowd reacted in a second and bodies tripped over everything getting off that porch. We scattered, and the bear continued toward the kitchen as calm and business like as ever. The cowboys had their horses tied by the cabin, and the horses spooked and bolted and jerked at their reins. Bob and Larry got to them and quieted them, then untied the lariats from their saddles. They got on one side of the bear and swung their ropes and ran the animal off up the hillside until he disappeared into the woods.

We watched the bear plod on out of sight, then stood in front of the commissary talking. The cowboys got ready to ride out, but Bob wanted a drink of water first. He swaggered around back and plunged through the screen door, then reversed and came flying off the steps. The bear squirmed out through the entrance he had fashioned two nights before. Larry rode after him on horseback, lasso in hand. The bear reeled and spooked all of the horses so that they stampeded wildly through the meadow. The cowboys reckoned there was nothing more they could do about the bear. Bob threw some fresh bait in the trap, then rode off to finish the day's work. Boss and the wranglers gave John a ride down to start the water pump on their

way out, and that left just Dave and me and Big Bertha
in Harlan. I was glad for the show the bear had put on.
Now there would be people to vouch that we had a
problem.

I didn't think the bear was through with us yet. Dave
and I wanted to try just letting him have the run of the
place. He might go in the trap without people staring at
him and bothering him and trying to rope him. Dave stood
watch while I put all of the food in the two refrigerators so
that the only food out was in the trap. I threw a few more
pieces of bread in the trap and took a broom and shoved
all of the stuff back near the bait sack. Then with everything set, we went in the other cabin to get some books.
We would walk over to the little ridge across the meadow
and keep an eye on things from there. Dave stepped out
the side door, gave a yell, and scurried out through the
meadow. I saw black fur and jumped back and slammed
and bolted the door, a wave of quick fever pulsating
through my body. Dave signaled all clear and I got out
the front door and across to the ridge.

The bear was back browsing around the cabin again as
soon as we got over to the lookout place. He wriggled back
into the kitchen and messed around for a while. He found
nothing to satisfy him in there and strutted out to the cage,
more at ease than before. He was very suspicious and
acted as though he had seen one of those cages before. He
stalked around and around it, sniffing, tugging at the wire
siding, checking the side panels. The bear stopped at the
doorway and put a paw up on the floor of the trap, then
withdrew it. Then he put his head and front paws through
the opening and inched a little way back into the trap.
John got back from the pump and took up watch from the
trees behind the cabins. Our eyes fixed on the trap, trying
their hardest to see the bear pull the bag and the door fall

shut behind him. Our ears strained to hear the heavy metallic clap of the falling trap door, but it would not come.

First the big bear grasped the garbage can liner full of scraps that Bob had just thrown in. He took it in his teeth and dragged it out of the cage, then spent several minutes pawing through all of its contents, scrutinizing every morsel for its value in satisfying his permanent hunger. When he had finished with it, the bear was less careful about padding back into the trap. There was honey-covered bread and lunch meat still lying on the floor. He stopped and lapped that up in no particular hurry, then moved a little further back, rolling his head around to sniff every corner of the cage. The animal found some fruit and pawed at it and played with it. He noticed the bait bag and sniffed at it. He licked it, then just swung it around with his paw. He grasped it in his teeth. WHONK! We had him! The bear spun around to the iron door. He paced the cage for a few minutes, then quieted down. We ran down yelling and laughing in release. We walked around the cage trying to believe it. We got our cameras and took all kinds of pictures with each of us standing by the caged bear. Whenever we got too close, the old bear would breathe steam and snort and bludgeon the sides of the cage with his brickbat paw.

Bob Knox was supposed to haul bears off as soon as one was caught. John took off down the hill to call him up. Dave and I set chairs out on the porch and spent the next hour watching our bear. The bear wasn't too concerned about his situation at first. As long as there was food in the cage he was happy. He might reach up and pull at the chain link sides once in a while, but for the most part he just stood in there with his head down in the bait bag, pushing it around the floor with his nose. When the food was gone he began more seriously to look for a way out. He pawed at the siding and twisted it around in his teeth. He checked the back wall and the top, then went back to the door. He pushed at it, then pawed at the bottom of it; a pipe across the floor on the inside hid the bottom edge of the door panel. Silly bear. Didn't he know these things were built by fish and game experts to hold his kind all night long?

Dave and I went about our work. There were still plenty of jobs to be done before Harlan would be ready to open. I had some things to do at my desk in the cabin and Dave was working up materials for his map and compass program. From inside we could hear the same innocent noises we had heard while we watched the bear out on the porch. We heard him keep pulling and tugging at the wire webbing sides of the cage. His claws would scratch down the rows of chain link and there were little metallic taps. WHONK!

"Hey, that didn't sound good," I declared in a Texas drawl that Dave aped for the next month. We ran outside to the corner of the building. "He's gone!" Dave shouted, and damned if he wasn't. We stared into the empty trap. All the enthusiasm of the catch drained away, replaced by a sickened feeling. We thought about Bob making a special trip up to get the bear, and about John, and how badly we all wanted to get rid of the old bear. The bear had left the trap running, because he sure wasn't around now. We looked the trap over again. The bottom edge of the door fit flush against the floor. The door was thick and heavy and solid. Except for one small hole. Claws. It had taken a claw caught on the spring pin hole to lift the door, a paw to wedge it up, and a little time to wriggle out. There was another hole in the door—one that lined up with the tube at the top of the trap so that it could be locked when the cage was closed. That made us feel sicker.

About suppertime Bob and Larry and John came driving up the road and we told them what had happened. They got out of the truck and we walked around the trap damning the critter and shaking our heads at the incredibility of the whole thing. The bear would not make the same mistake again, but we rebaited the trap and set it anyway. We spent the night in the commissary again, more uneasy than ever that the bear might be back and acting hostile. Bears had done that. But no bear came that night or any other for a long time. We moved back to our wall tents, not for bravery, but because there would be campers sleeping out in trail tents in Harlan, and we didn't want to hide from bears in the building while they slept on the ground in the open.

The bear stayed out of Harlan for a long time after his run-in with the trap. We had no bear trouble for several weeks, so Bob came and took the trap down to another camp that was having bear raids. Within a few days there was an upswing in dumped garbage cans and crude vandalism. John was handy with tools, and he spent one afternoon designing what appeared to be the ultimate bearproof garbage can. A steel brace clamped the lid down, held taut by tension cables attached to the side handles. In the evening one of us would have to take some time and secure the can for the night by a tedious process of wedging the brace through the cable's loops and across the can, edging it an inch at a time, then pressing the loops back to give some slack. The can was bearproof for two nights before the bears learned to work it. From that time on, the garbage spent the night in the commissary building.

One night we had barely snuffed the lantern and gone up to the tents when a barrage of raucous noises came from the kitchen. Chairs fell against the board floor and cans banged into the stove. A heavy blow pounded the floor. The big bear was back. The racket became a little subdued, then there was only the low rattle of chairs and the rap of the screen door coming shut. The noises lasted into the night, starting, stopping, then starting up again.

Dave went down to fix breakfast and called me to see what the bear had done. The bottom screen on one of the doors was ripped out again. Two chairs were turned over and silverware was strewn across the floor. Dirty, wet paw prints smudged the stove and refrigerator. The icebox stood open, the door wedged open against a straight-backed chair. Bits of food lay in front of the refrigerator and most of the food inside had been slobbered over. A plate of butter on one shelf was gouged by four deep claw marks. An empty, torn-up bacon wrapper lay near the door, and tracks and bits of paper led up the trail to the spot behind the latrine where more shredded ham and sausage wrappers were.

Bob brought us another trap, and as long as it stood out by the kitchen, Big Bertha never came around. We finally did catch one little bear who had played in the garbage regularly, but Harlan still slept light the rest of the summer. We couldn't forget the big one that was still out there—somewhere.

Cowboys are something else. Real cowboys, that is; not the gunsels who herd cattle in pickup trucks and smell more like English Leather than rawhide, but the smelly, dusty, lying, cussing, spitting, chawing, lariat-swinging cowpokes of the notorious American West. Although authentic cowboys are getting hard to come by, a handful of them still hold out on the ranches of Texas and New

Mexico, and if their breed is doomed to extinction by the grim reaper of technology, they would be the last to admit it.

Philmont had a few of this diehard breed, and although I got to know some of them pretty well, I could not truthfully say that I ever came to understand what made them tick. Philmont's ranges were ridden by such leather-faced cowpunchers as "Booger" Brown, "Boss" Sanchez, Leo Martinez, Sam Bennett, Bob Knox, and Larry Mesaric. These men spent most of their working days alone, and they built up their own ethics and values, free from societal pressures. There was a little of a philosopher in all of them, though any of them would have slugged me if I had ever said so.

That a cowboy never runs from a fight, takes meticulous care of his horse, shoots straight, and drinks hard, is well known to any TV nut, and it would be hard to refute any of those characteristics as legitimate parts of the cowboy personality. But they tell only a part of the story; for the screen artisans, eager to produce episodes full of action and glamour, emphasize these, and omit other traits and attitudes that are just as common among cowboys and that form a less-storied but just as sacred part of the Code of the West.

Maybe it is a little easier to understand the cowboy and his style of life when one is aware of his way of looking at things. A cowboy is satisfied with what he is and can think of nothing he would rather be. His only requirements are a good horse, an occasional bottle of whiskey, and a woman, probably in that order. The cowboy is proud of his occupation to the point of arrogance. He looks down on city bankers and politicians, and any other noncowboy. His feeling toward them is no kind of envy or contempt—he is just fortunate enough to have a better job than they do.

He is sure there is no more satisfactory occupation than that of the cowboy, and the annoying part is that he seems to be right. He is one of a very few in an urban-oriented America who is already secure and contented in what he is doing. For him, tomorrow's demands belong to tomorrow. Today is good enough. The cowboy puts in a backbreaking amount of work, but he does it all in his own time. Nothing ever has to be done right now.

Sam Bennett wrangled burros at Harlan, and it must have been an embarassment to him to have to live with three city dudes all summer. Sam was a homey mixture of buck teeth and manure and horse sweat. He had been chipping away at a college degree for seven years, and reportedly carried a can to all of his classes to spit tobacco juice in. Sam was a stockman all day and a goodtimer all night. He was also a master logician. Cowboy logic is incredibly simple, but it is also incredibly formidable. Its deductions may be hard to agree with, but impossible to refute.

Harlan only had one shower stall. I should say Harlan barely had one shower stall, for it consisted of but a leaky shower head mounted in an old canvas-walled latrine shelter. Its water heater was a curled section of pipe running through an oil drum. One of us would build a fire in the barrel every afternoon, and we would all wash up. Sam became indignant whenever he thought anybody was taking longer than necessary in the bath. He professed that no shower need take longer than a minute at the very most. He would say, "You can't wash everything but once. Once you've washed it, it ain't gonna get no cleaner. After that, you're just playin'." All of Sam's ethics were clear and unimpeachable.

There was a little ridge about a hundred yards from our cabin. It jutted out to a rocky point where there was a panoramic view of the whole of northeastern New Mexico. Someone was telling Sam about it and mentioned that he ought to mosey on up there and have a look sometime. But the cowboy made it plain that his boots were made for stirrups, not for walking. And if you had to climb a hill to get there, he durn sure wanted nothing to do with it. "If that horse can't get there," he drawled, "I don't need to see it."

I have never found a cowboy lacking in courage, but fairly often they come up short on brains. At the drop of a hat they will do things like flankstrapping burros to make them buck, then trying to ride them backwards. If a cowboy's eye strikes upon something that might be fun, he jumps up and does it, uninhibited by any pangs of good judgment.

Once we had a bear poking around in the vicinity of the Harlan cabin. He was not a cub either, but about the size of a medium grizzly. This bear could have feasted in our kitchen and then brushed his teeth with my toothbrush and I wouldn't have ever said anything to him. But it so happened that there were a couple of cowboys in camp, and one of them decided that he just could not leave without first roping that bear. He took out his lariat and followed the bear up into the brush, and started jockeying around for a good throw. Had the bear been in a nasty mood, Larry could have been shredded to very fine hamburger. But this bear's patience was exceptional, and it played along for ten minutes before unsheathing its claws, reeling toward the cowboy, and swatting at the air. In one of the few instances in which I have ever seen a cowboy in a hurry, Larry hurdled a scrub oak and came bowlegging it down the hill. I asked him later what he had meant to do with a big mean bear on the other end of his lasso. He nudged up the brim of his western hat and 'lowed that he hadn't given it much thought. He gave it some and then reckoned that he could have dallied the rope around a tree. Sure.

For all its rough edges, the cowboy's life is still an enviable one. It centers around the concerns that are most visible—his work, his play, his cattle. He may throw out a curse at the country's crooked politicians once in a while, but he's really a little too far from the mainstream of national and world events to get very worked up about them. He lives in relative isolation and likes it just fine. His air is clean, his water is pure, and he has no trouble with the neighbors, because he probably doesn't have any. The city fellers can have Wall Street and Sunset Strip and Washington. If a man's horse can't get him there, he don't need to see it.

By daylight we could look out over the mountains and down across the wide valleys that crumpled all around in hazy green folds. But when the sun paled and eased below the far peaks and night fell over Harlan, we sensed again the isolation, the deeply felt mountain solitude that set us alone in a wilderness place. Miles of dark mountain trail and wide stretches of the desolate flat country below and to the east separated our little post from the nearest human people. After sundown there would be no possibility of the sound of a jeep winding up the mesa's ruts. There would be no Rangers hiking through and stopping to guzzle water from our tank and to talk of the day. We were alone under the heavy enveloping night of dark ways and moody shadows and wind-rustled boughs and the night sounds.

We took care of things while there was evening light— washed the supper dishes and put the rustic shelves in

order, took in trail food packages from the camping groups
to keep them safe for the night, fastened the garbage can
lids down, hauled the flag down and folded it into a bulky
triangle. After dark the Scout leaders ambled over
dangling their coffee cups along, and we retreated into the
close cubicle of a cook shack to talk of many things while
the big porcelain kettle simmered full of water and coffee
grounds on a gas burner in the corner. The men sat around
the table on some straight-backed wooden chairs, and we
filled the narrow space that was enclosed by the board
walls and screen front and the wooden floor and the low
slanted roof. The night feeling filtered in through the
wide screen sides, and there was only the dim light that
glowed through the smoke-hazed chimneys of a couple
of lanterns to illuminate the faces of the mountain men.

The evening grew late and the men went off to find their
way back to their tents. We stowed away any food that was
out on the shelves, putting it in the old defunct icebox,
and blew out the flaming wicks of the lanterns, then
groped up the path that led to our tents up among the
trees. It was good to sink down into the warmth of a
flannel-lined bedroll and pull the open top close around
while the night chill swirled outside. Sometimes the forest
was still and quiet, save for the occasional rustling of pine
needles or the tap of a falling twig or pine cone against
the taut canvas overhead. But more often there was a
windy thrashing of the fir branches and the ripple of windblown tenting. On many of those nights we were startled
at the leaden metallic thud of a filled garbage can against
the ground, giving report to some bear on his nightly
prowl. After that dull crash there would be faint scrapings
and some random cluttered sounds that started and
stopped and went on forever while the bear foraged over
the contents of his kill.

The kind of night we had at Harlan was a strange kind
of adventure in itself. Out of the black loneness around
Harlan came occasional twists and turns that found their
way to the little mountain cabin where we were. When
that happened, it was up to us to do something, because
there was no one else to call out. There was no handy radio
that would put us in instant contact with headquarters and
its services. On a few of those dark summer midnights,
night travelers traipsed in through the outer country to
find us.

One night late in June we sat at our evening pastime
in the dinky shack listening to a squatty man from the
back hills of Pennsylvania tell about his exploits as an
herb hunter. He went on and on with stories about the
ways of the weird hill folk, all narrated in his own hard
Allegheny tongue that threatened to bray on each accent.
He was most interesting telling about what things the hill
folk did to strangers who ventured uninvited into the
hills without the company of one who was known and
accepted there. As ten o'clock came, though, we began to
wish he would run out of tales and head back to his camp
so that we could get to bed too.

Then there were voices in the dark from the trail west,
and three boys, open-eyed and gasping for breath, appeared at the screen. They needed a doctor fast for a boy
who was doubled up with chest pains and running a fever
at the Bench Camp. He had had some kind of rheumatic
heart disease before, and the leader feared it was heart
trouble now. The runners had stumbled across a six-mile
shelf land of seldom-traveled territory to reach Harlan.
The Bench Camp sat up on an isolated rim above Cimarron Canyon where groups passed through the middle belt
of Philmont. There was nothing much at the Bench, and
no staffed camp was nearby. Besides Harlan, the only

other reachable one was Cimarroncito, eight miles distant. Earlier in the afternoon, just before dark, three other boys from the same group had hiked over to ask for a full water can, saying that the spring at the Bench was dry and they had all gotten sick on water they took from the Cimarron.

I took down the specifics about the sick boy on a scrap of paper while John rummaged in his tent for a jacket and a flashlight. Then the two of us left Dave to put the boys up for the night, and we took off down the jeep road toward the phone station that was two miles down the mountain at the canyon highway. We jogged and walked and wound our way down the cloddy switchbacks, throwing a dancing beam ahead of us to break the night wall. We came to the rushing Cimarron and to the pale frame box that stood before it in an abandoned clearing. I worked the padlock on a back door and we entered the musty, dead room and walked across the dust and mouse leavings to the phone stand. I dialed up headquarters and raised a radioman at the Control Center. He put me on the line with one of the medics and I laid the story out for him. There was no road into the Bench Camp, so they would send one of the carryall vehicles through Cimarron and up the canyon. John and I would wait for them on the highway and ride with them up to a footbridge that marked the trail to the Bench. We hung up the phone and walked outside to sit on the steps and watch down the canyon.

We sat out in the mild midnight air for an hour or more, listening to the waters ripple and watching the shadowy mountain greenery waver in the night breezes. Finally the narrow, cross-eyed headlights of a jeep wagon puttered up the paved strip and we ran out to flag them down. John and I climbed in the high-riding cab and found places to pack ourselves in among the equipment and the three men who had ridden from headquarters. We started on up the canyon highway that severed Philmont. When we came into the territory near the cutoff, we began scanning the roadside stream for the small wooden bridge. We missed it entirely, then wheeled back around and edged down the highway, stopping every few hundred yards to throw a long beam on the riverbed. Finally we spotted the narrow log crossing and pulled off the pavement to park the wagon on a level shoulder.

One of the men from headquarters stayed with the vehicle while the rest of us took the steel-frame and chicken wire stretcher and started across the bridge and up the steep way to the Bench. I had hiked over to check the camp only a week ago and the others hadn't been this way, so John and I led carrying the stretcher between us. Then came John the medic, dressed in his whites and carrying a doctor bag, and following him was a Ranger carrying some blankets. The dark night hid the trail, and there were bends where we could only stop and probe around for it, but we could always sweep the flashlight around in a long arc and finally pick out some boot prints that were impressed in the deep, dry dust of June. We picked and walked and climbed, and finally we came up onto the Bench. We stayed on the path and soon a campfire flickered through the trees.

Three or four of the boys had the fire going while the rest of the group lay strewn around the fire in a lumpy patchwork of sleeping bags. One of the firewatchers pointed out the heart patient and the medic bent over and shook him awake. The chunky boy sat up in a shaggy stupor and John squatted down and began questioning him and probing his torso. The medic pulled a stethoscope from the bag he had toted along and fitted its terminals in his ears, then plotted several deliberate points on the boy's chest with the sensor. He gripped the base of the boy's neck and pressed into his diaphragm and asked how different things felt. When he was done, the medic concluded that the muscle spasms had been brought on by packstrap palsy, a painful kind of muscular ailment. He gave the kid some pills and told him what to do about the condition.

All of a sudden the urgency of this mission vanished, evaporating into the night gloom, and left us standing in a woody grove on the Bench, miles from anything that mattered. The stretcher lay discarded while we thought the situation over. There was nothing more to do, so the medic and the Ranger started off through the night, back down the mountain to their wagon. John and I stayed. The messengers who had hiked over to get us would need their packs when the rest of the group hiked on to Harlan for the next day's camp. We were in no hurry to get back on the trail anyway, so we decided to sleep there and carry the extra packs back in the morning. A couple of the boys got the extra bedrolls for us and we bedded down by the fire there with the rest of them. The sickness that the boys said they had gotten from bad water was real. During the night one of the good Scouts raised up in his sleeping bag, threw up to the side of him, pitched some dirt over it, laid down, and went back to sleep. He was on the trail.

When the night was gone, we were too. At first light John and I pitched some wood on the glowing coals and packed up the three extra packs and the rheumatic boy's pack. We each threw a pack on our backs and loaded the other two onto the stretcher, and started our tandem walk away through the morning and home to Harlan.

The last of several night capers happened in the late mid-summer. We were back where we always were in the evening, keeping watch in the cook shack. While we talked, three Scouts gusted in from up the meadow and bounded onto the porch. They had galloped along the path of an old jeep trail and down the side of Deer Lake Mesa to get help for one of their group who had taken a severe burn on his foot. The outfit was camped alone at a little meadow that was far from the beaten path, at a spring just above the stagnant pond of Devil's Wash Basin. The boys had been drying their newly rinsed clothes around the campfire when a nylon T-shirt flared. One boy went to put out the flame by stepping on it—barefooted. The burning nylon had seared into the flesh and stuck there on the bottom of his grilled foot.

For once we were in some luck. Sam had driven his pickup up to the burro pens and left it there for the night while he went back out with some wranglers. He left the keys with John in case anything came up. We put a flashlight on the framed map that hung in the cabin and plotted the best way to reach the trail camp. There was one possible way for getting in there with a good, rugged vehicle. There was the old, old jeep trail that passed near Harlan and wound around and up the side of the mesa, and along the rim to a point near the Wash Basin where it just stopped. It had been used a long time ago for access to some of the cattle country, but nobody ever went up there now. None of us had ever covered that trail either, but the boys who had come down it were pretty sure we could get over it.

We got in the truck and the boys piled on the back, and we took off down the road toward the Cimarron and away from where we needed to end up. We followed the long, lighted swath of the headlights down to where the old jeep road cut off through some pasture land below Harlan. We eased into its ruts and rode through the rim of meadowland that ringed Harlan on a lower terrace. We bumped across the pasture and started up the rocky, jagged groove that cut a scar up the side of Deer Lake Mesa, John driving, me navigating, and the boys jumping out to open the barbed wire gates along the way. We weaved up the mile of long switchbacks and climbed a long rut that brought us up onto the mesa. John kept the truck in low gear and muscled the steering wheel to hold us in the bumpy groove and away from the long drop-off that sloped down and away from the road. We came onto the level top of the mesa and followed the headlights' beam through the forest and its undergrowth. Branches grew out across the path and we rolled over little saplings that had taken root in the old road.

At one point the road seemed to dead-end in a heavy wooded grove. There was good trail behind us, but no apparent place to go in the dark jungle grove we were facing. We took the flashlight and climbed out to look around for any trace of a road. We looked the little area over, then, without bothering to face the same direction, we began to size it up.

"This doesn't look too bad," I opened.

"It doesn't look too good either," John returned. "Uhhh-uh. I'm not going any farther. This is it."

"It's not all that rough," I contended.

"Yeah," was his mock assent. "That'd only tear the bottom out of Sam's truck. No way."

"Well, you can tell it went that way. We can drive straight over those saplings."

"You call that a sapling?" John retorted, and I turned to where he was motioning in the other direction toward a cluster of mighty timbers. Getting our heads together, we settled on the way ahead and got back in to drive deeper into the night wilds. We rumbled on for a half hour and finally came out of the timbers and into a little meadow where the peaked trail tents stood around a low fire in the distance.

It was a good night and the boys were out around the fire in a bantering mood. The leader stood by the path, very glad to see us, and we eased on across the meadow and parked the truck by him. The barefoot boy was sitting over by the fire, not bad off, but he had sure done a job of welding the nylon material into the sole of his foot. We wrapped some loose gauze around the foot to keep it fairly clean while some of the others got his camping stuff together. We unwired a bale of hay that was in the pickup and spread the straw around the truck bed, then loaded the boy on and rolled away to find our way back down the tedious, weaving rut.

In time we made it across the mesa and back down the nerve-clinching switchbacks and onto the Harlan road. We rode on down toward the Cimarron and John stopped at the phone station long enough for me to call headquarters and tell the medics what we were bringing them. We bumped over the bridge timbers and cruised over the smooth highway to town, then turned toward headquarters and rolled over the road and in through the service lane to the health lodge. The medics were up and getting ready to go to work. We turned our boy over to them, then headed for a lighted window across in the chaplain's quarters, there to hit the priest for his jeep can full of gas that would get us out through the dark country and back up to our mountain place.

6

We set up down at Abreu this summer and it was good to be back there, back by the running waters and back in a part of the country I already knew as an old friend. Abreu looked pretty much the same, but there were some things changed too. The pump was repaired and there was even a pipe to the cabin. The river bed was cleared of most of the timbers and logjams that had cluttered it. There would be no supply base in the big room of the cabin where we had run one before.

No other camp could match my staff, either for ability or

for variety. Bill Shopp was the Range Officer and next in charge at Abreu. Clint and Brooks were a couple of rifle instructors on the way to military careers, ROTC cadets. They would never take on a job and get it done; they would "cover down" on it and get it "squared away." Brooks liked to read and was usually attached to a copy of *Marine* or *Patton*. Ever so often Clint felt duty-bound to put the fine military spit polish back on his black army boots that could get so scuffed looking in a week of camp life. He would get them out on the front porch along with his saddle soap and a bucket of water and scrub and polish them until a glossy shimmer came into the smoother faces of the old cracked leather; then he was right with the world again. I was afraid for a while that Abreu might have the country's only hunter safety course that included bayonet practice, but at least that never happened.

Bill Haggart was the western lore cowboy. Then there was a white horse and a Labrador pup we called Ol' Blue. Blue spent the day wrestling with dishrags or rummaging through our tents looking for socks to hijack, but in the evening he became a deer dog. When Blue discovered deer grazing in our meadow he would set up on point and begin stalking. He would run at them barking a bark that he was not completely sure of. Sometimes the deer would scatter to the hills and Blue would run them out of sight, then come loping back to the cabin grinning and wagging his tail. But once in a while the deer would hold its ground and stand taut, with a hard glare in its eyes toward Blue. Then Blue would skip around and run and stop, throwing out a bark now and then. A few times the deer got the upper hand and charged, flashing its sharp hooves at Blue's heels. The dog would run yelping for the cabin and decide that he wanted to go back to being a puppy for the rest of that evening.

Finally there were a pair of flycatchers who nested in a beam on the porch and raised two families in front of our door. Most of the summer the mother seemed not to mind the traffic under her nest. She would just wait until no one was closer than three or four feet, then slip in with a bug for one of the open beaks. But on the days when a brood would begin to learn to fly from the nest she was fierce about strafing anyone who came near the porch.

Besides having the rifle range session, we were a western camp. On the porch we nailed up posters of outlaws who had ridden the country around Philmont. Bill Haggart's saddle rested on a log by the door and his chaps and spurs hung on a nail against the cabin wall. In the mornings Bill would have the groups out in the meadow where he would show them all about a cowboy's horse and equipment and what he did. Bill would tell them about the old trail drives and the days of the open range, how Philmont's cattle ranching was done now, about how the cowboy's job had stayed the same and how it had changed down through the years. Then he would show them how to rope and teach them a little about how to handle a lariat themselves.

The only drawback in any of it was Bill's horse. While the rest of Philmont's wranglers rode spirited mounts with names like Don Juan and Thunder, they sent Bill a white plug named Shorty Knots. Shorty was a stumpy old packhorse with two sprung knees and the mentality of a mule. His back swayed and his sagging belly wobbled from side to side whenever Bill could bring him to a trot. Bulging veins stood out on his chest and legs. Fortunately, all Shorty's job required of him was that he stand around twice a day and look like a horse, which he almost did. Usually he would go about half-asleep during the programs, and then Bill could raise up and stand straight up in the saddle and talk from there for a while, so most of the boys went away impressed anyway.

In the evening we had a western campfire, and that is where we could really function. That is where we were a team. We had an array of songs and guitar playing and stories that could have gone all night, and we executed a campfire that fired up just about any imagination that sat in front of it. A little before dark we would get on our cowboy clothes and Brooks would get the campers up to the place and light the fire. Then the rest of us would take our guitars and I'd take my banjo and we would stroll out across the meadow to the campfire and strike up. The three or four of us sat around on some big sections of logs on one side of the fire. Sometimes the first-day groups would hike over from the starting camp across the hill and we would have more than a hundred boys gathered around. Bill was a terrific storyteller and he could make Dodge City and Abilene come to life for them. We kept a branding iron in the fire and when it shimmered red, Brooks would tell them all about branding and then sear a "T" into one or two of the logs. Then Clint would tuck a wad of Beech Nut tobacco in his jaw and reel out a tale about Black Jack Ketchum and his gang—how old Black Jack came to rob a train close by and got into a shoot-out with the law in a canyon up in the north country, then finally got himself hanged and decapitated over at Clayton in the 1890s. Out there under the stars we had some of the best times of the summer.

This was a particularly heavy year for Philmont, and Abreu got pretty harrowing sometimes. To start with, we had a lot of program duty. The rifle program was a hunter safety course that took four hours a session and often went both morning and afternoon. Bill always had at least one or two western lore programs, then at night there was always the campfire to do. And after that we always had the leaders in for coffee. The flow of Scout groups was more constant than I remembered it ever having been before; once the summer got into full operation we hardly ever had fewer than six or eight groups a night. In addition to these there were usually a few groups in the starting camp that was nearby.

We had a horseback ride bringing boys up from Rayado every day and another one taking last-day campers out. Since Abreu was one of the main camps, there were staff and Rangers hiking through every day; and since the Rayado was full of trout, people from headquarters often came up to fish. A covey of wives came up from the training center across from headquarters each week and parked their Buicks and Oldsmobiles in front of the cabin while they walked up the road to look at rocks. That burned us up. The only trouble with all of this was that we could never really go home from work. Whenever we weren't giving a program we were checking groups in and out or selling fishing licenses or cooking or cleaning up. And when we weren't doing any of those, people would always be coming in and going out, and it was hard to have any time of our own because we lived there.

Because it was that way, we started to appreciate and look forward to the occasional times when we could get off and work at something without being vulnerable to interruptions or just relax without having to be conscious of representing anything other than ourselves. Those were the only times we could work at a job and finish it without somebody coming up and wanting something. They were the only times we could kick things around and be at ease, and there were not enough of those times. One of them happened on a morning when the groups left early and there was no program to give. Two new latrines had been built over in the campsites, and the old ones torn down. It was up to us to clear the wreckage and clean each area up. We had come to like manual labor and were glad to have time to get at the job. Brooks and Clint and I took claw hammers and went across the creek into the woods and had a great time tearing up those old latrines. We banged away at the boards and ripped up the roofing shingles with feeling. We threw the boards in a pile to be burned. The unburnable debris had to go too, so we started to go back and get buckets and carry it all back across to the garbage cans until we thought of the space left in the old latrine pits. That was one of the small pleasures of the summer—me and Brooks and Clint throwing shingles down a crapper all morning. Clint took the old metal urinal, hammered it like a wild man, pounded it flat, and we threw it down there too.

Some nights the coffee hour would drag long, so we would start brushing our teeth and setting mousetraps and bolting windows. As soon as the leaders got the idea, we would turn out the lights and wait until the men's flashlights disappeared into the woods, then open back up and get out a pie or something and open the floor to levity. Once in a while a night was too warm and still and clear to let it go by unappreciated. When that happened we would walk up the chapel hill and look out over our camp or go up to the corral where we could look out toward the lights of a little town far to the east. Or we would just sit out in the middle of the meadow and talk for a long time. Whenever we had a chance to stop and think about it, we could really like being the Abreu staff.

The C.B. radio peered over my shoulder and squawked its noontime trivia while we ate our lunch. I swallowed the last corner bite of a peanut butter and jelly sandwich, then turned to take the microphone from where it stayed wedged between two nails on the cabinet.

"Abreu to Control."

"Stand by Abreu—go ahead Apache." Apache Springs always had lots of important business with which to fill Philmont's airways, so I started on a Hostess Twinkie. I could have finished off a half dozen.

"Control to Abreu—go ahead."

"Is there any 10-49 for us? Over," I recited. There rarely was a message for us; that was just our way of checking in. Sometimes I would get tired of hearing their metallic "Negative Abreu," and would just ask for a 10-36—a time check—instead.

"10-4," the box blurted. "Your 10-49 concerns an Expedition 719K that will be traveling through your camp. Please allow them to charge the rifle safety course, fishing licenses, and any other costs necessary for participation in Philmont program. Send a record of charges made to headquarters and costs will be paid through their local council. This procedure has been approved by Joe Davis. Over."

"10-4, anything else? Over."

"Negative. Over."

"Thank you, Abreu clear."

"Control clear." I set a note on top of the radio with the rest of the messages on hand for reference and went on with my business.

On an evening later in the week I checked over the list of groups supposed to be coming in for the night. One had not showed up yet, and if it didn't come in before another hour, I might call in to report them missing. The sun backed off beyond a mountaintop to the west and dusk fell over the canyons. The Abreu gang was getting

ready for our nightly campfire fandangle—putting on
cowboy clothes, tuning up guitars, laying the fire.

A confused band of wanderers appeared on the northern horizon up by the horse corrals. The ragged line
staggered down a shallow draw, drew up to the cabin, and
sprawled over the camp. There were twenty boys and a
leader, each headed in a different direction. Two Rangers,
showing the wear of a long day, were coping to hold them
into some kind of group. The whole thing collapsed on
the porch, victim of a treacherous four-mile hike, all
downhill. They all dropped their packs right where they
happened to be when the Rangers said they could stop,
creating an instant salvage yard. The packs were lopsided-
looking globs of bedroll and clothes and food, all tied up
with a couple of random loops of cord and hanging by a
prayer onto the pack frames that had been furnished at
headquarters. There were pots dangling and axes laced to
the packsacks, and at least one pack had met disaster a
couple of miles back. It came in as a pile of loose rubble
in the arms of a drippy-nosed, onion-faced boy, to be
dumped in a pile on the porch. As soon as they had had
their fill of Rayado water, some of the boys slumped onto
the porch while the more energetic ones went looking
for the soda fountain and asking if the bus was here to
take them back to Newark. It was their second day on
the trail.

The boys seemed to have no sense of what they were
supposed to be doing or where they had been or where
they were going. They displayed no feeling for the time
of day, and no regard for authority, except when the
leader would threaten an unruly one with a fisted blow.
Each boy's pocket carried a moldy, folded up trip plan
that had been thrust at him in headquarters and whose
lines and words told the places he would go and the

things he could do for the ten days, but it was foreign and meaningless and forgotten. The boys did not look much like what you would call a group. It was more of a jumble. It wasn't as though they were flouting the orderly ways that we expected, they just weren't aware of them. The boys were seeing Philmont from within their own world of experiences, a world that was as unreal to us as Philmont's was to them. They were full of questions.

"Are we gonna sleep in that house?"

"Say, do you have a car?"

"Is this here where we gonna eat?"

"Can we swim in there?"

"How big are those horses we spozed to ride?"

"Hey, do we gettin' to sleep in some beds tonight?"

Philmont was not really a good time for them. They all wanted to go back home.

I went out to meet the leader. He was supposed to be twenty-one but looked more like eighteen. His main qualification as advisor for the outfit seemed to be that he was bigger than the rest of them. The real leader, who had come out on the bus, had decided to forego the rigors of the trail, the evaporation of a two thousand-mile buffer zone having dulled his exhilaration for mountain camping. Anyway, when I found the trail leader, he was reeling around the porch, rolling his head up and around as he raved softly.

"Ooah. . . . I am so sick, I am so tired. I want to go home. Where is that bus? Say, will you take me back down to Philmont?" So much for leadership. After a time he recovered enough to ask about the swimming pool, canoes, and horses he had been told he would find. "Oh man," he said, sinking into disappointment, "you mean there ain't no swimming pool here?"

719K was the well-meant idea of someone who wanted to help some economically disadvantaged boys, but didn't know just how to go about it. Probably the organizers could think of no more exciting and beneficial experience than camping in the mountains, and certainly it had been that for many boys. But in trying to do something worthwhile for these boys, the people had failed to see the differences between diverse neighborhoods and ways of growing up.

Philmont's planning booklets emphasize the rugged nature of trail life and urge leaders to plan in advance and prepare their groups, or else forget about taking on the rigors of the trail. But in their hopes for the downtown boys, the organizers had overlooked that and sent the boys on their way, certain that they would have a good time and learn a lot of new and interesting things. Boys were collected at random off the streets, and any boy of the required age could come, whether a Scout or not.

As it turned out, few of the boys who made the trip had known any Scouting at all. Most of them had never slept in a tent or rolled a sleeping bag or cooked over a fire or hiked. They had never been taught any of the things they need to know in order to make it here, and they weren't too sure what it was they were supposed to like about the place anyway. Most of the boys had identical sleeping bags, all new. The same was true of their boots and packs. They had been outfitted from scratch. But despite every good intention of the organizers, the project turned out like so many others of its kind. Because the people who wanted to help knew too little about what they were doing, the result was frustrating for everybody and the ones being helped ended up the losers. The boys found themselves stumbling around in the mountains miserable and far from home, a perfect setup for others to look on and talk with scorn about how ungrateful these lazy rascals were not to appreciate what they had been given.

Because of the obstacles that are evident in trying to make one program of activities work for everybody, Scouting is devising inner-city programs which are based on the particular interests and needs and resources of inner-city neighborhoods. Through these newer activities popular Scouting programs have been built in some inner-city areas, and maybe through one of these new programs, the Newark organizers could have come closer to accomplishing what they wanted to do. The present dilemma was that these boys hadn't gotten the chance to start at the beginning or to pursue Scouting through their own natural interests.

Never minding that the group didn't belong here to begin with, I began to think how we might make this day or two in Abreu worthwhile to them. We tried to think of some activity we could do with the boys that might just spark their interest. There had to be, we thought, enough basic common denominators among people that we could make ourselves understandable to the boys and see what was making them go. We never really found a way though. Thinking about it depressed me, because I could see what the problem is when people from different cultures want to work together and trust each other, but don't have the slightest insight into each other's reasons for being like they are.

In any encounter I ever had with any of the boys, I never felt that we were on the same wavelength. Our thoughts just didn't meet up. We looked across at each other eye-to-eye, but never saw. About the closest any outsider came to rapping with any of them during their whole stay at Philmont was when the leader of one of the other groups in camp, in referring to the English founder of Scouting, asked one of the boys if he had ever heard of Lord Baden-Powell. "Nope," he returned, "but I heard of Adam Clayton Powell." And as for us, it was hard to be at ease working with the group when part of our minds was on the known and unknown threats they seemed to represent. Although we would sometimes see individual attributes that would give some particular boy a little of his own personality apart from the others, the temptation was to lump them all together and wonder at the circumstances by which the boys had come to be as they were. They did take an interest in the program that we called Hunter Safety and they more candidly called Shootin' the Guns, and despite our qualms, the rifle instructors set up a program for them. I walked up to tell them about it and to see how they had survived a drizzly night.

The Newark boys were camped in one of my favorite camping spots in Rayado Canyon—on a flat, wooded bank just above the riverbed, close to where the river came splashing down spread shallow across the rocky floodplain. Up the canyon and across the stream were towering dark pines, and the hulks of Philmont's steepest mountains stood beyond. But when you walked off the trail and down through the trees into the group's campsite, there was no doubt about it—you were in a disaster area. Hanging in limp folds from fir branches were the new sleeping bags, mud caked, wet, and gunky. Most of the tents stood feebly, their guy ropes tied to anything in reach and their sides sagging somewhat pitifully. Ground cloths, watery on both sides, had slid far out from under the tent sides. Inside the dank tents lay dumped over packs and wads of damp, mud-stiffened clothes. My mind started wandering and I thought of what it would be like staying in one of those tents and wearing those clothes and hiking out with the rest of them. I imagined having what I saw— if these were my bedroll and my boots and my jacket and all. No way, I said. It was too much. I would have thrown everything away and started over.

Under the fireside tarp was a pile of mud-spattered trail food packets—food for the next three days—the plastic sacks ripped asunder and their contents vandalized by their owners, who had forgotten about tomorrow's lunch in the haste of getting at what could be eaten right now. If it wasn't eaten now, who was to guarantee it would be there later anyway? A puddle ringed the campfire and the two Rangers crouched there cooking breakfast, having long since given up on teaching the boys to do it themselves. The camp was engulfed in loud noises and confusion. Threats and defiance broke the bantering atmosphere. I stood around for awhile, trying to look at ease and to show that I could fit in with anybody, but the place was too close and too unsettled. I told the Rangers about the rifle program, then got out of the area.

Getting the boys through the rifle program took up most of the morning, but the riflemen went slowly and drilled hard on the safety rules and kept their eyes glued to the firing line. Things went well enough. Only one boy was reckless enough to be sent back to camp; the rest of them did all right. The rifle instructors came back down to the cabin glad that it was over and feeling lucky that nobody was shot. As we finished lunch though, Mike Jarvis walked in and poured out a box of two or three dozen live rounds of .22 caliber ammunition, some of which had been handed over to him by one of the boys. He had heard a shot and gone over to where some of the boys were throwing the live shells against rocks. We mulled it over for awhile, and finally arranged another program to get the boys off to another part of camp. Then we had a little shakedown in the campsite, going through all of the packs and all of the tents until we had collected the rest and could be pretty sure that the only ammo in camp was locked up in the range house.

The Director and the others who ran things in headquarters knew all about the disoriented group that had appeared at Philmont a couple of days before, and they were keeping their fingers crossed and ears cocked toward Abreu. They checked with us by radio now and then to ask how things were going. Mr. Dunn wanted to know whether the Rangers were running into any physical danger, which was not an unreasonable thing to wonder about.

It soon became clear that a ten-day pack trip was not going to work with these boys. Somebody would just have to take that in and do something about it. After supper Control radioed out to give us the plan they had worked out. Tomorrow the boys would have a horseback ride down to Rayado, where they could look through the Kit Carson place before being ferried on a bus to Cimarroncito. At Cito they could ride out the rest of their trip without the burden of having to hike and pitch camp every day. They might get into some good programs devised for them and make some day field trips, doing things that they could already do or could learn in a short time. A black professional Scouter would come to Philmont to try and give them some leadership.

Breaking camp and packing up was a tedious job for the Newark boys, and they spent most of the morning at it. I had started up the road to see how they were coming on when a small boy rounded a curve and raced toward the cabin. He was crying furiously and churning the ground as fast as his bulky army boots would let him. I stopped him and he blurted something before two bigger boys caught up to him, snorting and cussing. "Don't you hit me, don't you touch me," the little one shrieked. His eyes were wide and full of terror. One of the others cuffed him to the ground, but I pushed the older one off. The little guy jumped up and they cussed each other again about who ran off without doing any work. I glanced down at a small, tight fist clutching a knife close to his jeans, the blade hidden behind his leg, and a thumb twitching at it. His bigger friend was also clasping a knife between his thumb and fingers, but hadn't opened it yet. The one really not knowing what to do was the outsider who stood between them. I wasn't sure whether to yell at them, get out of the way, or go for my knife too. The other three had a common language, and they at least knew what was going on. But I didn't know anything; I couldn't make much headway at finding out what the problem was. All I wanted to do was to get this bunch out of Abreu without any of them messing it up with their blood. I ran the little fellow down to the cabin for safekeeping and everyone kept his blade clean for the time being.

When it was nearly time for the horseback ride, one of the boys came down to tell us they were ready. I walked back up with him to do the usual check-out routine. A couple of them followed me back and forth through the trees where we searched for paper on the ground. The Rangers had done a good job and there was nothing much, maybe a plastic bag and a couple of band-aid wrappers. I looked at the sump where they poured out soups and greasy liquids and dishwater. The screen over it was clean and there was not much for flies to be drawn to. They finished putting out the fire and declared that it was ready for inspection. I looked around for a stick and began digging through the soggy bed of coals. I pawed back and forth through the ashy mound, stopping here and there to press my palm on it to check what seemed to be a hot spot. I stirred back and forth and turned up furrows, and stopped to pick out a can lid and a few bits of foil. All of my digging produced maybe half a handful of trash bits.

While I worked, a couple of the boys watched over my shoulder. One of them broke the silent watching to ask, "Why do we have to take that out—I mean, what does it hurt for it to stay in there?" I looked up at a face that wasn't defying anything. He was just standing there watching and wondering why a grown person would be squatting down in the mud stirring through a bed of coal mash and picking out flecks of tin foil the size of his fingernail. So. After going through all of this a half dozen times a day for four summers, somebody had finally asked me what I was doing it for, and at this particular time, I didn't have anything to say back to him. If he had been rebelling at cleaning up the camp because I said to, I might have let it roll off. Or if he had been a good, dull Scout whose dad sold insurance and lived in a suburb, I would probably have had a good, dull answer ready for him. But the question just occurred to him, and he thought I would have some reasonable explanation for what I was doing. I looked up meaning to answer him, but whenever something came to mind, it didn't seem to fit, and a sense of futility come over me again, a feeling that seemed to apply beyond the situation at hand. Finally I muttered something about having to keep the wilderness clean so the next campers could see it that way too. Neither of us was too impressed about it, and I soon wished I had just not said anything.

The boys hoisted their packs up but they weren't groaning so much this time; they wanted to ride the horses. They started out down the road and I followed them down, pretty much within myself and feeling a little defeated at having lacked the sensitivity to build any kind of rapport with the group.

I couldn't recall ever having seen any ghetto-type neighborhood whose appearance was worth fretting over. I mean, if everything that is supposed to work is broken and there are rats running around under the bed and you are looking for the money to pay last month's rent, what's a handful of trash in a hidden grove up in some mountain range? Maybe such pastoral beauty is a luxury for people who eat three times every day, and maybe aesthetic concerns are for people who have nothing better to do. These boys were wearing secondhand clothes, given to them or bought with what was left of a welfare check or a handful of hard-gotten bills. They had never been around anything that deserved the tender care that suburbanites give their lawns and cars and furniture and clothes—and wilderness areas. They had grown up in a world where such things were far away and meant for someone else. I wondered if they could imagine anything more ludicrous than somebody looking for lost pieces of trash.

A week or two into August we began to feel the end of the summer coming on, and while it had been good to us, most of us would be ready to get back home and back into the other kind of living. We had all been doing exactly the same jobs, giving the same talks, going through the same routines every day of the week for what seemed like a long time, and we looked forward to a change of pace. Clint was itching to get back down to A & M and get the Aggie band squared away. Brooks was figuring rides and airline schedules to Georgia. I would be starting into a new city and a new pursuit myself, and I was anxious about getting at it.

At the same time, those last summer days were some of the best and most enjoyable ones of all. It had been a rigorous summer, a busy one, sometimes a hard one. But as the season moved into its last couple of weeks, many of the pressures and people that had kept us in motion evaporated away. Finally we were able to see the country and enjoy its quiet mountain feeling again. We had time to hike around and look around and take care of our own projects and correspondences that had been neglected so many times in the rush of things. We had a chance to know the people in the groups that camped at Abreu each day, and to listen to them.

A week before close-out Brooks came back out from a day off and brought with him some fine red sirloin steaks, each an inch thick and bigger than any plates we had to serve them on. On the last night that we would all be there together we fixed everything up and had a final banquet celebration. We set up a long table beneath our canopy up in the trees and built a good oak fire nearby to grill the steaks. We put on our best Scout clothes and feasted on steak and salad and baked potatoes and cheese-cake, and then I made a kind of a speech to let the boys know they had done something good. Afterward we got into our cowboy gear and lit in for one more time around on the show that had been our pride—one last lying, tobacco-chewing, banjo-picking, super, wild west, four-log campfire. We got the boys settled around there and sat around on our old familiar stumps and put out our best bunch of wild songs and old-time stories.

One more time we sang out "Old Joe Clark," and one more time Bill laid the days of the open range out for two score wide-eyed young believers. Once more Clint stood in the light of a fire that burned from a high blaze to a glowing bed of coals while he talked, and railed about the Folsom train robbery. We had, over the course of the summer, gotten to look pretty natural in the varied outfits of dusty boots and dirty jeans and bandanas and cowboy hats that were our evening duds, and we had gotten to feel pretty much the sense of the old times we told about. Although we had done the whole thing a jillion times, we were listening to ourselves a little extra this time. There wouldn't be another one like it.

In the morning Clint packed up and was gone back to Texas where he needed to get underway setting up for school. The next day Bill Haggart was gone too, bound for California, and there were three of us left. Soon after lunch Mr. Clemmons came navigating up the road in an old faded Chevy that he kept for easy jaunts out into the hills, and he brought us a Ranger we knew and thought a lot of to help us finish out the summer. We had all been itching to turn cowboy and we split up the duties of Bill's western lore job. Between chores and programs we took turns riding Shorty Knots wherever we could get him to go around the canyon. We fed him and curried his mottled white back and doctored his sores and gave him more attention than a worn-out packhorse would ordinarily know what to do with.

There were a lot of things we could do now that we couldn't do during the busy part of the summer. When we knew exactly where our groups were, or would be hiking in from, we would sneak off and plunge into the deep, clear pool of icy water that we had staked out up the river. The dank, drippy showerhouse that we had could not compare to a refreshing soak in those forbidden waters. We worked hard most of the day at getting the camp ready for closing, then lazed the late afternoons away in the breezes under the canopy if there was nothing else to be done. We enjoyed Abreu for once.

Day by day the camping groups dwindled in number and the smaller and more isolated camps were closed out. Finally Philmont was a Scout ranch of two or three open camps and a few last expedition groups. Across the mountains were two dozen camps whose tent sites were untouched, whose water pipes were drained empty, whose windows were nailed shut against the coming winter, and whose floors were sprinkled with rat poison to preserve the cot mattresses until another summer. The radio box that had chattered so incessantly now hardly ever spoke. The road into camp went untraveled, and we were by ourselves.

On the last night of camping three crews of California boys hiked in and we had Abreu going full throttle for them. When they were set up, Brooks and Bill took them up to the range for the afternoon of gun safety and target shooting. We set the old campfire aflame for one last time under the stars, and even with a two or three log cast we could still generate the excitement that attached itself to those older days. Afterward the boys headed down across the bridge and back to camp yelling lines they had picked up from our stories. We dashed out the fiery red bed of coals and took the leaders over to the cabin where Bill Shopp had the old aluminum coffee pot going on the back burner. We visited along for awhile before the day's hiking effects set in and the men started down the dark path back to their campsites.

We still had work to do if we were going to be ready to pull out tomorrow afternoon. Bill and Brooks set up cleaning and oiling guns in the big room and we worked on until after midnight. When we were packed and set, we sat back and put away a quart of milk and an icebox pie that we had put by for just this occasion. Then we got our towels from the tents and took a flashlight, and hiked up the road to soak off a long day's grime in the river pool. A little past the showerhouse we left the road and picked our way through the dark woods and toward the rushing sound of the creek. We stripped in the cool night air and laid our clothes across a boulder that bounded the deep eddy.

Bill and Brooks plunged in and winced at the chill of the mountain waters. I took a few cautious steps myself and worked my way into the frigid pool. We crouched in and treaded the chill pond, trying to generate warmth that wasn't there. Bill and Brooks were out and in and out again, but I eased around over the coarse, sandy bottom to a place where the river poured in through a chasm behind me and where the water was comfortably deep, and there I settled in. I thought the chill would wear off some, but it didn't, except in a numbing sort of way. Still the current felt good and I sat suspended in it for a half hour or more. My mind had lately been on the times ahead, and it turned there now.

The future, beginning with tomorrow, was very uncertain, and I would be taxed for sure to work it out. I had decided on graduate school, but was not sure even now where another day would find me. I had in applications at three schools, all of which would begin before I could get there, and I had gotten no word of admission to any of them. I hadn't thought a lot about what I wanted to study either. I had no acceptance papers, no job, and no place to live. Tomorrow there was a camp close-out with its ten dozen things to remember to do. After that I would have to drive all night to get to a campus by opening day, and after that there would be the hundred details of getting settled in. These last days had been a good quiet time before a long round of hassles, and this was the last relaxed time there would be for a while. So I just sat there and let the chilly waters ripple and let the light cloud fleece drift across over the country that had grown into me so. Bill wondered at my arctic-like physiology. Brooks dried himself off up on a rock and declared that the boss was "old army." But I sat in a little longer, not that the pool was so comfortable, but because there would be many times in the days ahead when I would think of the summer life, and wish to be there.